Beyond the Tithe

Giving Without Guilt

by

Valerie R Jackson

Beyond The Tithe: Giving Without Guilt

Copyright ©2016 by Valerie R Jackson

Printed in the United State of America

ISBN-13: 978-1533126894

A Christian Bible study by Off-Kilter Bible Studies

www.offkilterbiblestudies.weebly.com

Cover design by Graphics.tif

Printed by CreateSpace, An Amazon.com Company

Dedicated to all the

Off-Kilter Bible students

who love His Word.

Beyond the Tithe:

Giving Without Guilt

Table of Contents

Beyond the Tithe

Preface

Should I tithe? Dare I not? That was the puzzle.

Having gone through a divorce and the resulting dive in household income that most women experience in such instances, I found myself supporting myself along with one, then two, of my late teens and early twenties children. It wasn't going well.

I had moved from the flat desert landscape of Abilene, TX to Charlottesville, VA in the forested foothills of the Blue Ridge Mountains. Having been a military wife up till that time with three children, I had been employed over the years in fits and starts wherever we were stationed. I had been to college, yet I didn't have any clearly marketable skills. But I had gained some experience in retail.

As we struggled to live on my income, I resolved to tithe. I was in full blown "I can't afford *not* to tithe" mode. My net income and the child support money for one nearly grown high school student covered my excess of bills and the rent. What it did not cover was food, clothes, or even toiletries.

You need to understand that my lifelong background was as a military dependent. My father had been in the military and so had my ex-husband. That was the world I knew how to navigate. There was no concept of how to get help in the civilian world or even an idea that anyone was prepared to give it to me. Social services? Food pantry? Isn't that for people with no money at all? Besides, I couldn't even begin to figure out how to access programs like that.

Our clothes, which I didn't have the funds to replace, were slowly being worn to tatters. Basic things like deodorant and socks were really hard to work into the budget. And that list of required school supplies you get at the beginning of the school year? Hoo-boy!

I ate two for $1 candy bars for my lunch at work. There was rarely any food in the house besides toaster pastries. To this day, I'm still not sure what my son lived on. Church fellowships became an opportunity to feed my children a real meal.

I hadn't even conceived of the idea that my church might provide financial support to a member. I grew up in the church. And I'd been to multiple churches and even several denominations as I moved from military base to military base, and state to state. So far as I knew, no such ministry existed. If there was one, it was invisible to me.

You have to understand my mindset. I was the resident adult. As far as I was concerned, taking care of my household was entirely my responsibility. Not my family's, not my neighbor's, and not the government's. And according to what I had learned in the church over several decades, I couldn't afford *not* to tithe! If I tithed I was told God would take care of me, and I needed all the help I could get. If I did not tithe, things would never improve for us. So I tried my best to get 10% of my income into the offering plate whenever I got paid.

As a Bible teacher, I both knew and had taught the doctrine of tithing. But as I struggled to take care of us, I never saw our circumstances getting better. I felt like a fraud. So I thought the situation over and finally came to the following three possible conclusions.

Conclusion one: God's word was not true. (That idea was simply ludicrous. I'd lived with Him too long, and so immediately discounted that theory.)

Conclusion two: What I had been taught about tithing was not true. (Hmm. Interesting idea. Nah!)

Conclusion three: I was missing or misunderstanding some vital principle about tithing that, when fixed, would cause God to shower me with financial blessings. (Entirely possible.)

Since I was unsure, I resolved to re-examine the scriptures on tithing as if I'd never seen them before. No preconceptions were to be allowed. I was to attempt to look for the plain sense of every scripture I examined, and not insert interpretations or assumptions about what the verses *really* meant.

I started with pure scripture, pulling up every verse I knew of and filling a notebook with my scribblings. Then I started digging into the background. And the result of the study surprised me. I thought, "Hunh! That can't be right." And went on with my life.

Several months later I decided to give it another shot. I came to the same conclusion, yet somehow still could not believe it. It was not until my third time through that I finally said, "Okay, God. I both see it and believe it now. This is the way you want me to walk."

I write this book now, not because God has brought me into a life of glorious material riches. He hasn't, in case you're wondering. I write it because I learned things that I think would help others who struggle with these same issues. Being a tither can be hell. Being a non-tither can be hell. I've been both.

My biggest problem with modern day giving was tithe-guilt. The most potent form was the guilt I felt because I wasn't tithing. Never mind I wasn't even putting food in the refrigerator. Quite obviously, I scolded myself, if I went back to regular tithing God would see that all our needs were met.

Other forms of tithe-guilt I experienced in my life included guilt because I was tithing but perhaps wasn't giving the *whole* tithe. I had been taught that meant 10% of the gross of whatever I was bringing home in my paychecks. But what about the child support? I wasn't giving any of that. It was covering most (but not quite all) of the rent every month. Maybe God wasn't blessing me because I didn't include that, too. Perhaps there were other funds I was holding back on somewhere and didn't realize it.

Then there was guilt because I quite obviously was not at the level of faith God required me to be at. I knew this because everyone knows that "without faith it is impossible to please God."[1] And since, when I did manage to tithe, there was no blessing returned to me probably because I was lacking the faith to receive it, it was also equally clear (to myself, at least) that I just didn't have enough faith to please God. Positive spiritual affirmations just didn't seem to affect the level of faith I was feeling.

There was also the "Yes, I'm tithing but my children's clothes are ragged and we're eating cheap food and maybe if I wasn't tithing I could take better care of my family" sort of guilt. So I felt guilty for tithing. But, I also felt guilty for not taking better care of my children. No win.

And the "I'm trying to tithe but my husband doesn't want us to tithe and most of the tithe is from his paycheck, not mine" guilt. Do I obey God? Or keep my husband happy? And do I have the right to tithe on household money I myself didn't earn?

There was also the "Sunday School is having a lively discussion about how we all need to tithe," and I'm going to sit quietly and nod like I'm tithing too. But I'm not. And that brings on guilt. Because I'm not a good enough steward of my money to tithe. Or because the household keeps needing stuff. Or maybe because (gasp!) I just don't want to give that much of my money.

---

[1] Heb. 11:6

And then there's the good old testimonial-guilt. Apparently everyone but myself had a story about how they once didn't tithe, but then they decided to start giving God 10% of their gross income, and within a week, they were promoted and given a raise. Or given a new (free!) car. Or received an unexpected refund in the mail.

Whether I tithed or not, stuff like that just didn't happen to me. My position at work didn't change. My paycheck didn't change. I drove the same car for 13 years until I drove it into the ground. "Am I doing something wrong?" I pondered. "Is God using poverty to punish me for not putting enough money in the plate at the church?"

I had been told that if I didn't tithe, a curse would be on my finances. Yet, based on my life experiences, when it came to tithing I was, quite literally, cursed if I did, and cursed if I didn't. It was no longer about if I tithed. I just wanted my choice to not come with a boatload of guilt.

It is possible that I'm the only believer in Christian history subsumed with tithe-guilt. But just in case I'm not, I wanted to create a non-scholarly resource that might help others who were struggling with the same questions. I wanted to present what I learned without pounding a viewpoint about whether you should or should not tithe into the reader's head from the very beginning. (I really hate when others do that to me.)

I did come to a conclusion, but will wait to the last couple of chapters to spell it out. By then you will see how I got there. But what I really want is to get my fellow believers to a place of peace, one where they also can make their own decision on tithing and give without the tithe-guilt.

The scope of the book is to not only look at tithing as it is described in the Bible. I want to compare it with today's teachings on giving. What does the Old Testament say? Okay, I got that, now what does the New Testament say? Though this is not primarily a historical account, I was also interested in how the tithe has been viewed throughout the history of the church. Tithing has obviously changed since Deuteronomy was written. How? When? Why?

And what about tithing today? On what sources of income do those who tithe give, and how is it given? And equally important, does it really matter? How prevalent is the doctrine of tithing in the modern church? I know what my primary denomination teaches about it. Do other churches teach the same thing? What about Christians in other countries, much less around the block? Is this just an American thing?

This isn't a scholarly thesis by a theologian. Neither is it my goal to cover every mention of tithing in the Bible. Rather I want to take you to the Scriptures that had the most impact on my understanding.

To ease reading, I paraphrased some of the passages of scripture and placed most scripture references into the page footnotes. If you are interested, you can use the footnotes to look up the verses for yourself.

I used the English Standard Version of the Holy Bible for its modern day readability and its goal of creating a literal translation of the original text. Your Bible may translate the text in a way that seems to offer a different understanding of the scripture. It's all part of what makes the Bible fascinating, so don't let that discourage you from digging further.

What I hope by the end of this study is to encourage my fellow believers to respond to the doctrine of tithing with knowledge that is not driven by hype. And by doing so, to be able to give confidently through their freedom in Christ.

Chapter One

Tithe Reasoning

As I examined the role of tithing in the Christian life, I wondered why people make the choices they do in regards to giving a tenth of their income toward the church. Even those who agree on whether to tithe don't necessarily agree about the appropriate motivation behind their actions. I have also noted disagreements about what exactly should be tithed, how it should be given, and to what purpose.

I searched the internet for what Christians believe about tithing. I also searched my own heart. At those points in my life when I did tithe, and those points in my life when I did not, what was my rationale? I don't mean the reasons I told people that simply parroted what I had been taught. I wanted to dig into what was going on with my conscience at the time.

In the end I came up with 6 reasons why Christians tithe, and 6 reasons why they do not. I believe most explanations fall into one of these categories.

6 Reasons Why Christians Tithe

1) **Their particular church or denomination teaches that they should tithe.**

If their church teaches the importance of tithing, a believer is more likely to tithe, or at least believe they should be tithing. In other words, tithing does not seem to be a practice that believers stumble upon due to independent study. At some point, tithing was introduced to them as a doctrine.

I pondered, "Do churches teaching about the tithe influence a believer's decision to tithe?" I performed a minor survey on an online Bible forum to help answer this question. At the time of this writing, 30 people responded, so it was hardly comprehensive.

The majority of the respondents, 80%, agreed with their church on such teachings and tended to follow that lead. In fact, as of this writing, I had a 50-50 split, with 40% being tithers because their church taught them to tithe, and 40% being non-tithers because their church did not teach tithing. 16% did not tithe, even though their church taught it. And only one person, 3%, tithed even though their church did not teach it as a doctrine.

It seems to be rare for someone to belong to a church that did not teach tithing, yet he or she still chooses to tithe. I would need a much larger study to see if my percentages hold. It was a little more likely that someone belonged to a church that taught tithing, yet rejected the belief. In the latter case, the believer had the opportunity to consider the doctrine of tithing for themselves. Some agreed with it, and others did not, and their actions reflected their beliefs.

2) **Tithing is an act of obedience to God.** They see evidence in the Bible that God instructed his followers to tithe, and so they do so. Such believers are often motivated by their love of God and their gratitude for His blessings. Some believers, however, give because they feel God commanded it, and they feel guilty if they do not because they believe it is God's will.

14

3) **Tithing is a means to acquire wealth.** Their ultimate purposes for that wealth may be positive (build God's kingdom, take care of my family, etc.) or negative (build my own kingdom, live large, etc.) But their giving is motivated primarily by the expectation of a perceived future reward.

Some believers' perceive tithing as a resource that might produce more money towards living expenses. Their ultimate purpose may be simply a desire to earn a reasonable living. Once that reasonable standard of living is attained, they may also desire to have enough left over to give to others without putting their own household at risk. They have a heart to give, and deeply wish they also had the resources.

A third reason a believer may desire financial gain is because they see it as evidence of God's favor. They believe that their lack of money is evidence that they are doing something spiritually wrong or that they lack sufficient faith. To be financially well off is visible validation of their faith in God and of God's approval. Therefore, they strive for it.

4) **Some churches make tithing a ministerial requirement.** This is particularly true for churches that require their workers to tithe as a condition of leadership or employment.

For some churches, tithing is viewed as evidence of spiritual maturity. Others present it as simply being a good example to the congregation. In either case, the issue of whether to tithe is effectively taken out of the giver's hands. If they desire to serve, then they tithe.

5) **Some believers simply love to give.** They may not have the resources, but they certainly have the heart. If they are wealthy, they give generously and often. If they are not wealthy, they are frequently willing to go without in order to give as their heart desires. Tithing is an extension of their inner drive to provide resources where they see a need.

6) **Some believers tithe for practical reasons.** They realize that church operations and missions can get expensive. Since their

desire is to support the church and spread the word of God, they find tithing a sensible way to do so.

6 Reasons Why Christians Do Not Tithe

1) **Their particular denomination or church does not teach tithing as a doctrine.** They do not tithe because the issue has never come up. Other forms of giving may be encouraged instead, such as pledging a certain amount annually to support the church and its goals. Or their church may depend on freewill offerings.

2) **Some Christians are heavily in debt.** They do not tithe due to large and possibly unexpected expenses such as medical bills, or because they are drowning in credit card or student loan debt. They are already treading water and have a very real expectation of going under if they try to squeeze anything else out of their income.

3) **A believer's spouse does not want to tithe**. In this instance, the spouse is either another believer who sees giving in a different light or a non-believer who sees no reason to give up 10% of their earnings to the church.

This household does not tithe because while one spouse believes in the importance of tithing, they are not willing to tithe off the other person's income without approval. In addition, the believer may not want to make financial choices that affect the whole family without a consensus. The driving desire is to maintain the peace of the household.

4) **Some people have never been exposed to the teachings on tithing.** Perhaps they are still learning the gospel. Or they could be intermittent church attendees; those who have been believers for a long time but somehow have never been at

church or bible study when that particular doctrine was brought up.

5) **Some people believe tithing is a false doctrine.** The reason they do not believe God requires a tithe from the church today is two-fold. First, tithing is seen as part of the old Covenant whereas our relationship with God is based on the new Covenant. Second, they see tithing as a law that only applied to the Israelites while they still lived in the land of Israel. Tithing was only valid for the Jews when they had a Temple to present tithes and offerings.

6) **Their income is insufficient to tithe.** Introducing a tithe into this person's budget would be detrimental. They may or may not desire to tithe. But when they compare the minimal needs of their household with their actual incoming resources, they don't see any logical way to make it work without cutting necessities.

What and How Christians Tithe

When I examined what Christians choose to give, I noticed a diversity of beliefs. By definition, a tithe is a tenth or exactly 10% of something. Christians differ in how they define that tenth. I know you're thinking, "How many ways could there be to define what is essentially a mathematical fact?"

The real question is, "On what income or percentage of that income does God, or my church, require me to tithe? Do I tithe on *everything* I earn? Everything I get? Or everything I have?" Those whose hearts desire to give to God, often desire deeply to give a correct tithe.

Most tithers give money. There are some, however, who choose to also give measurable or immeasurable intangibles such as time, skills, or material goods.

The following are internet quotes which I believe are representative of what, why and how Christians choose to give to a church or other Christian organization. Most provide scriptural references for their beliefs.

Tim Greenwood Ministries -

"God claims the tithe is His.

30 'And all the tithe of the land, whether of the seed of the land or of the fruit of the tree, is the Lord's. It is holy to the Lord.' (Leviticus 27:30 NKJ)

The New Testament says nothing to change God's instruction on tithing. The tithe is holy and still belongs to God."[2] (www.tgm.org)

Growing Your Church - "Christian giving comes out of an understanding that all of our financial resources like everything else that we have, comes from God. It is a gift, not for hoarding, but for continued use in building up the Kingdom of God. (www.growingyourchurch.com)"[3]

Berni Dymet - "In fact, the moment we start applying 'the law' to the grace and the freedom that we now have in Jesus Christ, then we are cursed:

For all who rely on the works of the law are under a curse; for it is written, "Cursed is everyone who does not observe and obey all the things written in the book of the law." (Gal. 3:10)"[4] (www.adifferentperspective.org)

---

[2] Tim Greenwood Ministries; http://www.tgm.org/WhyUShouldTithe.htm
[3] Growing Your church; http://growingyourchurch.com/45/fivereasons-christians-should-tithe

Pastor Jim Feeney, PhD - "1,500 years after Moses received the Law, Jesus REAFFIRMED in His day the validity of tithing:

Matthew 23:23 Woe to you, teachers of the Law and Pharisees, you hypocrites! You give a tenth of your spices — mint, dill and cumin. But you have neglected the more important matters of the law — justice, mercy and faithfulness. You should have practiced the latter, without   neglecting   the   former."   www.jimfeeney.org[5]

Grace Ambassadors Bible Fellowship - "The most popular tithe today is the tithe that went to the Levitical priesthood (Num 18:21). There is no Levitical priesthood today." (www.graceambassadors.com)[6]

Getting confused? So was I. No matter what side of the argument you are on, you can find both teachers and scripture to validate your position.

One fairly comprehensive source is an article from Tanzania on "The Right Way to Tithe."[7] I include it as an interesting view of the many

---

[4] Berni's Blog, http://bernidymet.com/why-i-dont-believe-in-tithing/

[5] Pentecostal Sermons and Bible Studies; http://www.jimfeeney.org/tithing.html

[6] Grace Ambassadors; http://graceambassadors.com/prophecy/law/reasons-to-stop-tithing

[7] Universal Church of the Kingdom of God;
http://uckgtanzania.org/index.php?option=com_content&view=article&id=23&Itemid=501

ways people choose to give because it covers almost every way one can tithe. This article conveys that everyone receives some sort of income, whether you are a business person, a housewife, or even if you are unemployed. You must be living on something. Therefore, everything you get should be tithed on, with the tithe going to the church (as opposed to charitable organizations or directly to the needy).

The author advocates setting aside 10% of what you receive before you deal with bills and other expenses. They also differentiate between tithes (the 10%) and offerings (anything beyond the 10%). Even if you are a beggar, 10% of what is gifted to you should be returned to God.

This writer holds a strong belief that not only does everything belong to God, but tithing is God's requirement of us. The believer is to tithe everything that comes into their hands or which is for their use. What's more, they believe that we are under a curse until we fulfill this requirement. (At one time I attended a church where it was taught that the whole church was under a curse because of non-tithing members. The teachings of this article draw from similar beliefs.)

"The Right Way to Tithe" tries to clear up the natural complexities that derive from this approach by answering questions such as the following: If you do not yet tithe, what do you do about resources already in your possession? In other words, do you back-tithe?

Does a business owner tithe from their salary or their profit? If you're unemployed, how do you tithe? Suppose you're on a pension? Suppose you took out a loan? Suppose you sold your house? What about employment benefits? Suppose you're homeless?

The author declares that "If you don't receive wages, you will probably receive other forms of income such as gifts, allowances, government benefits, occasional business, etc. You must tithe these."

I am not sure about government regulations in Tanzania, but in the United States, I must caution you that it is illegal to use certain government benefits for purposes other than indicated. For instance, if you receive food from SNAP, the Social Services government food assistance program, what you have received is solely for the use of the household which applied for the assistance.

Yes, you can set a plate before someone you invited over to your house for dinner or bring a dish to a potluck. No, you may not purchase food and give it to your church's food pantry or your equally needy neighbor who you are concerned about. Such distribution of your resources can result in the loss of your own benefits.

Equally comprehensive is the eHow article "How to Tithe."[8] The idea here is that you tithe on everything you have, and the teachings of this article quite naturally flow from that premise. In this case, they are less concerned about the details of how to turn income into a tithe, and more interested in defining what "everything you have" means.

The believer is expected not only to return to God 10% of their monetary income but also take into account non-monetary resources such as time (bible study, volunteering), blessings (an abundance of food or clothes), talents (tutoring, cooking, babysitting), connections and other resources. In essence, if it is within the sphere of your control, you should tithe it.

I'm a little curious as to how you offer 10% of what is not truly measurable. I suppose if you are tithing your time you could understand that 10% of 24 hours is 2 hours and 24 minutes. So that much of each day should be devoted to God's work.

Tithing an abundance of clothing, however, becomes problematic for me. At what point can I consider myself owning more than my household needs? Do I pare back to the minimum required for daily living, then give the rest? Which articles of clothing do I choose to give away? The best? The surplus that no one is actually using? And where should I donate them to make sure they go to God's work if my church doesn't collect such things?

---

[8] http://www.ehow.com/how_4919387_tithe.html

When it comes to tithing things like talents and connections, all circuits in my brain fry completely. Do I factor in the time and training it took for me to attain the level of competence I have in order to determine real world value? Or do I simply tithe my time concurrently with the talents and skills I possess and have both accounted as two for one? If I'm a doctor, do I offer 10% of my time to provide free medical services to fellow church members?

I am not being facetious. For myself, this is a dilemma of practicalities. Math has never been my strong point and I have always found figuring out 10% of a dollar bill to be a fairly simple process. Anything more complicated is going to be a problem for me. I shouldn't have to hire an accountant in order to give to my church.

On the other side of the coin are those who just as firmly believe that tithing is not mandated for the Christian church. And their arguments are often the flip side of the same verses pro-tithers use to support the giving of tithes.

For instance, in Gen. 14:20 there is an account of Abraham giving a tithe to Melchizedek, a priest of the Most High God. This event happened prior to the giving of the Law of Moses.

Those who support tithing point to this passage as proof that tithing is still required because it pre-dated the Law and therefore is not included among the laws that were made obsolete by Jesus' crucifixion and resurrection.

Those who reject tithing as a doctrine for today use the same passage to point out that Abraham's tithe was a one-time event and not an ongoing practice, and is therefore not relevant to the tithing which was mandated by the law at Mt. Sinai.

To sort out for myself exactly what the Bible does and does not say about tithing, I started with the Bible itself. And Genesis.

Chapter Two

The Tithes Before the Tithe

This is not meant to be a comprehensive review of every mention of tithing in the Old Testament. However, there are a few key passages that must be looked at. I will examine them first because they are frequently cited in both defenses of and in arguments against the principle of the tithe. Second, because understanding them will help to shed light on our topic.

The Curious Case of Melchizedek

Since the account of Abraham's tithe to Melchizedek in Genesis 14 is the first mention of tithing in the Bible, it is a good place to start. This account of a tithe being given takes place before the tithe is established in terms of the Law of Moses. Both those who support and those who reject tithing mention this event, but with different interpretations.

The Pro-Tithing argument is founded on two pillars. The first pillar identifies that Melchizedek is a *type* or *shadow* of Christ. Therefore, the giving of tithes to God / Jesus is modeled here for future believers.

A *type*, in theological terms, doesn't mean Melchizedek was a pre-incarnate Jesus or even an early version of Jesus. It means Melchizedek was a person whose life pointed strongly toward the Christ who was to come.

The second pillar points out that since tithes were presented by Abraham to the High Priest Melchizedek prior to the giving of the law to Moses, the custom is not affected when the institution of the New Covenant displaced the Old Covenant. Tithing is not strictly speaking an Old Covenant concept, it is much broader than that and so still applies to God's people today. This is in much the same way circumcision remains a Jewish custom even if they are Messianic Jews.

Acknowledging that the New Covenant supersedes the Old Covenant indicates a knowledge of the chapters in Hebrews discussing Jesus and Melchizedek.[9] If one believes the book of Hebrews is Scripture, which pro-tithers certainly do or they wouldn't bother to cite it, even indirectly, then what is discussed there must be taken into account and explained in regards to beliefs about Abraham's tithe to Melchizedek.

The Anti-Tithing argument is also based on two pillars. The first explains that this tithe was an isolated incident. There is nothing in the Scriptures to indicate tithing to the High Priest was a custom at that time. To be fair, neither does it indicate that such tithing was not a custom. The scriptures are silent on that point, and other historical documents would have to be examined.

That the custom of tithing existed at this time does seem clear from the narrative, even if there's no explanation in the Bible as to who generally tithed to whom, or upon what occasions. In other words, did the pagans also tithe to their gods, thereby making it a cultural custom? Or was this solely something done by believers in the Most High God?

---

[9] Heb. 6-7

The second Anti-Tithing pillar declares that tithing, along with other forms of proscribed giving to God, was completely abolished at the cross. Therefore, this incident, while interesting, is considered irrelevant to a discussion on whether one should tithe today.

Abram meets Melchizedek

Now that we have a general idea of the viewpoints regarding this passage of scripture, let's take a look at these verses to see what they actually do, and do not, say.

For context, we need to look at all of Genesis chapter 14, and a couple of verses in chapter 13. Up until now Abram and his nephew Lot had been traveling together. As time passed, however, both men increased in riches to the point that the land was not able to sustain both of their households.

There simply was not enough land to feed not only their huge flocks and herds, but there wasn't room for the tents and shelters that the people in their households lived in. By mutual agreement, Lot moved his entire household to the plains of Jordan, near a city called Sodom.

At this time, five kings lived in the plains, including the king of Sodom. The others were the kings of Gomorrah, Admah, Zeboiim and Bela (Zoar). For twelve years, these kings had been subject to Chedorlaomer, king of Elam in the north. But in the thirteenth year, they decided they weren't going along with that anymore and rebelled.

The king of Elam, along with three other northern kings, promptly went to war against the kings of the plains. And Lot and his household were in the thick of it.

Well, the four kings from the north won the battles and, by way of recompense, took everything that belonged to the kings of Sodom and Gomorrah. They made off with their goods, their food, and all of their people, leaving them not much of a kingdom. And poor Lot and his entire household got swept away with them when the northern kings departed for home.

One member of Lot's household escaped, however, and brought the sad news to Lot's uncle. Abram promptly armed 318 servants in his household (I told you the households were huge) and set off to get his relatives back. By the grace of God, not only did Abram bring back Lot, he brought back everything Lot owned, everyone in Lot's household, and pretty much everything the northern kings had made off with, even that which belonged to the kings of the plains.

From here we begin at verse 17.

"After his return from the defeat of Chedorlaomer and the kings who were with him, the king of Sodom went out to meet [Abram] at the Valley of Shaveh (that is, the King's Valley).

"And Melchizedek king of Salem brought out bread and wine. (He was priest of God Most High.) And he blessed [Abram] and said,

"'Blessed be Abram by God Most High, Possessor of heaven and earth; and blessed be God Most High, who has delivered your enemies into your hand!'

"And Abram gave him a tenth of everything."[10]

These few verses are the entire passage regarding Abram's encounter with Melchizedek. There are a few notable things about this King of Salem. First, he wasn't involved in the war yet he received a tithe of the spoils. Second, while we tend to think of Abram as the sole follower of the Most High God during this time, Melchizedek is introduced as a priest of God Most High. There is obviously a lot more going on culturally that we just don't know.

---

[10] Gen. 14:17-20

26

And finally, Melchizedek pronounced a blessing over Abram, and Abram in response gave the priest of God a tenth, or a tithe, of all the goods he had recaptured. Just as the kings of the north had, by rights of conquest, held ownership of all they had captured, Abram held the rights to what he had brought back and could distribute it as he wished.

This is seen in verse 21 where the king of Sodom tried to dicker with Abram, asking just for the citizens of Sodom back. Without the people, he really didn't have a kingdom. Presumably, they could restore the rest over time.

As the victor Abram was welcome to keep the rest of the goods if he wished. To his credit, he gave everything that had previously belonged to the king back to him with the exception of the tithe already given to Melchizedek, and what the young men had already eaten. He did not include the men that fought with him in his generosity, however, and asked that they are permitted to keep the portion that was rightfully theirs.

I find that these four verses are insufficient for either camp to prove their viewpoint. For those who support tithing, just because Melchizedek is identified as a type of Jesus isn't reason enough to declare that future Christians must offer tithes to Jesus as Abram did to Melchizedek. It just seems to need more to firm up their argument. Likewise, it would take other scriptures, perhaps somewhere else, to argue what if any effect the establishment of the New Covenant has on the symbolism of this moment.

As for those who reject the idea that even today we must tithe, again there is not enough information here to either agree or disagree. Yes, in scriptural terms this seems to be an isolated incident. But without knowing for sure if this tithe was a custom from the surrounding cultures, a reaction to events, or something Abram did on a regular basis anyway, it's hard to draw conclusions as to just how isolated this incident really is.

Fortunately, this is not all the Bible has to say about Melchizedek. For a more thorough explanation from the Judaic viewpoint, we need to look at Hebrews.

A Transformed Priesthood

While the bulk of the discussion of the priesthood of Melchizedek and how it relates to the Christ is in Hebrews 7, for a fuller understanding of Christianity and the Law of Moses you pretty much have to read all of Hebrews. However, the focus on Melchizedek begins with the last two verses of chapter 6, which reads as follows:

"We have this as a sure and steadfast anchor of the soul, a hope that enters into the inner place behind the curtain, where Jesus has gone as a forerunner on our behalf, having become a high priest forever after the order of Melchizedek."[11]

Keep in mind that part about Jesus entering the Most Holy Place as a forerunner on our behalf. You'll need that thought later.

Chapter 7, verses 1 and 2, are a review of the events we just read in Genesis with an expansion of the description of the king of Salem. Melchizedek is "first, by translation of his name, king of righteousness, and then he is also king of Salem, that is, *king of peace*.

"He is without father or mother or genealogy, having neither beginning of days nor end of life, but resembling the Son of God he continues a priest forever."

This is not to be taken literally, as he was definitely a human being. Rather it indicates that contrary to custom, the Scriptures make no mention of Melchizedek's lineage. Neither does it delineate the start or end of his reign. His priesthood is neither marked by a beginning nor concluded by his death. It just is.

In verse 4, the writer points out that Melchizedek's importance was apparent by the fact that Abram tithed to him. Indeed, the future priests of Israel, the sons of Levi, also tithed to the king of Salem in that they were still in Abram's loins as his unborn descendants at the time. (vs

---

[11] Heb. 6:19-20

5-10) The Levite tribe, which themselves receive tithes under the Mosaic Law, in a sense paid tithes through Abram and so showed themselves subject to Melchizedek.

Even though Melchizedek's descent is not counted from the tribe of Levi which are the priests of God, this particular priest received a tithe from Abram and then blessed him because Abram possessed the promises of God. And so verse 7 says, "It is beyond dispute that the inferior is blessed by the superior."

Why is this significant? Because the importance of the Levitical priesthood has always been recognized. It was under the Levitical priesthood that the people of Israel received the Torah, or Law, or Teachings of God.

Verses 11-12 give us a huge boost in understanding this. If perfection, or the goal, was reachable through the Levitical priesthood, what need would it be for the order of Melchizedek (Jesus) to replace the order of Aaron (father of the Levites)?

In other words, the New Covenant, administered through the priesthood of Jesus, which has key similarities with the priesthood of Melchizedek, has now replaced the priesthood of the Levites. We are then told, "For when there is a change in the priesthood, there is necessarily a change in the law as well." (vs. 12)

Does the law hinge on the priesthood? Or does the priesthood hinge on the law? Either way, the priesthood and the law appear inextricably linked.

This presents a better argument for those who believe the tithe has been abolished. If a change in the priesthood (from Levitical to Messianic) causes alterations in the law, then a change in the priesthood (from Melchizedek to the Levites) would likely have caused a change also.

The question is, from priesthood to priesthood, exactly what portion of the law might have changed? Here I have to say that "change" might be better understood as "transformed." The law of Moses wasn't deleted in its entirety and replaced with a new one. Jesus himself declared that he came to fulfill the law, not abolish it.[12] So we need to take him at his word.

According to David H. Stern, author of the Jewish New Testament Commentary, Hebrews 7:12 "is the only place where the New Testament speaks of a transformation of Torah." "The context makes it overwhelmingly clear that no change or transformation in Torah is envisioned other than in connection with the priesthood and the sacrificial system."[13] He argues that the original term "implies retention of the basic structure of *Torah*, with some of its elements rearranged ("transformed"); ...

If the modern Christian can somehow wrap his mind around the idea that tithes aren't really money, they could also argue that tithes could be considered part of the sacrificial system and not solely a means of provision for the priesthood. Lambs and goats do have to die, after all.

Even if every single point of the sacrificial system between the Melchizedek priesthood and the Levitical priesthood didn't change, there certainly was a huge change between the Levitical priesthood of the law of Moses and the priesthood of the Christ.

This is the key change: *Because Jesus became the final guilt offering, there is no need to offer any other sacrifice for sin.*

Ah, but a tithe isn't the same as a sin offering, right? No, it isn't, but it needs to be kept in mind that Hebrews points out that Jesus' death and resurrection really did bring about a change in the law. And we know tithing is certainly part of the law, even if it existed before the law was given.

As Christians, we can't logically remain obedient to a law that has changed. But neither do we want to run afoul of being disobedient to a law that has remained the same.

---

[12] Matt. 5:17

[13] Stern, David H., *Jewish New Testament Commentary*, p. 681.

Hebrews 7 talks about tithing, but it is in regards to the Levites and in regards to Melchizedek. In regards to Jesus, it neither confirms nor disavows tithing under the new order of priesthood. The priesthood of Jesus supplanted the order of Aaron and brought us beyond the curtain and into God's presence. This is the most important thing to take away.

Subsequent chapters go on to explain how the New Covenant under the new High Priest in the true tabernacle is superior (meaning better for us) than the Mosaic covenant under the Levitical high priests serving in the old tabernacle.

The reason it is better is because Jesus became the forerunner to ourselves one day being able to go into the Most Holy Place of the true temple and meet with our God. It is better because Jesus offered the once and for all sacrifice of himself for our sins, and humanity no longer needs to continually bring the blood of lambs and goats before God to atone for their sins.

Upon conclusion, it appears those who believe the tithe has been abolished may have a better case in linking Melchizedek to their argument. But it's hardly an airtight case. There's not enough evidence that the tithe Abram gave was anything more than a one-time event prompted by the circumstances.

The importance of knowing the law changes when the priesthood changes, however, should be kept firmly in mind as evidence that the giving of the law to Moses made the Melchizedek priesthood moot.

Jacob: The Other Tithe before the Tithe

One can hardly argue Melchizedek's pre-eminence in that he tithed prior to the establishment of the Law of Moses without having to cover Jacob's tithe, too. Yes, there is a second instance of tithing before Israel became a nation. And as determined Bible students, we can't just ignore it and wish it would go away simply because it doesn't agree with our personal theology. So let's gird our loins and take a look.

Jacob's story is a nice long one. It runs from his birth in Genesis 25, fights its way through all kinds of family drama, winds its way through an exile, a love story, and a lot of trickery, and then finds its way, first back home, then all the way out to Egypt, not giving up the ghost until chapter 50!

The part we are interested in comes after he has been sent away from home to prevent his twin brother from committing fratricide, but before he meets his uncle Laban and his family. This is the "Jacob's ladder" story in chapter 28.

Before he left home, his father Isaac passed on to Jacob the blessing which God promised Abraham.[14] As Jacob was traveling, he stopped to spend the night on the road. Literally. He just lay down right where he had stopped, and used a stone for a pillow.

As he slept he had a dramatic dream. A ladder was set up on the earth with its top reaching all the way into the heavens. Angels of God ascended and descended upon it, and at the very top stood the Lord God.

> God told Jacob, "I am the Lord, the God of Abraham your father and the God of Isaac. The land on which you lie I will give to you and to your offspring. Your offspring shall be like the dust of the earth ... and in you and your offspring shall all the families of the earth be blessed. Behold, I am with you and will keep you wherever you go, and will bring you back to this land. For I will not leave you until I have done what I have promised you."[15]

Jacob has not, so far as I can tell, done anything to merit God's attention and protection. In fact, his life up till this point was not anything to be proud of. Jacob woke up from this dream more afraid

---

[14] Gen. 28:3-4
[15] Gen. 28:13b-15

than anything. When he got up the next morning, he set up a stone memorial and vowed a vow to the Lord.

> "If God will be with me and will keep me in this way that I go, and will give me bread to eat and clothing to wear, so that I come again to my father's house in peace, then the Lord shall be my God, and this stone, which I have set up for a pillar, shall be God's house. *And of all that you give me I will give a full tenth to you.*"[16]

Now, I find this fascinating for all sorts of reasons, but primarily because it fits no "rule" of tithing I have ever heard. First, God promised Jacob not only offspring but protection both on the trip out and on the trip back. He promised not to leave him.

In response to this great gift of grace, Jacob responds with a vow of his own. Now, upon first reading, it seems conditional. It seems that Jacob puts the burden on God for protection and provision, and only upon God fulfilling his role would Jacob agree to tithe. But upon further meditation it reads more as an act of faith.

Jacob believes in advance that God would do just as He promises. He believes God's word. There is no doubt in his mind. God did not require a tithe of him before promising to take care of him, nor did he stipulate one afterward. Neither is God's blessing a reaction to anything Jacob instituted.

Jacob's immediate response to this divine largesse is gratitude. He certainly doesn't have much now, but offerings he will make in the future will continue to express both his belief in God's faithfulness, and Jacob's thankfulness for God's love.

What is more, Jacob declares "And of all that you give me I will give a full tenth to you." This is actually beyond the requirements of the future law of Moses, which only asks a tithe on the annual increase of crops and herd animals. Not "all that you give me."

---

[16] Emphasis mine

I am not even quite sure what to do with this passage. But it does tell me that tithing, or any sort of Biblically-based giving, will not necessarily fit into any preconceived notions of mine. If I am complex, surely my Creator is even more so.

Chapter Three

Dining at the Lord's Table

The seasons have turned. The crops are in, the cattle have calved, and the lambs are grown strong. Your storehouses are full with the fruits of a year's labor. There is plenty for the household as well as the marketplace.

The owner of the vineyard has gathered his grapes. New wine crowds the cellars. Grapes are dried and raisin cakes - moist and dense in their richness - have been carefully wrapped and set aside for the future. The shepherds' flocks have increased, both the sheep and the goats.

There is meat for now and throughout the coming winter and spring. Cheeses, both pungent and mild, have been made of the milk. The farmers have gathered their grain; wheat, barley, and corn. Flour has been ground, and hot, fragrant loaves have been pulled from the ovens.

This is the time of year you step back and take inventory. This is the time of year you nod and smile in acknowledgment; God has done it again! The land is full of foods from which only His hand has the power to provide; the unfolding of a seedling and the miracle of new life in a womb.

This is the time of year. God has invited you to dinner. And not just you, but your family and your neighbors, the poor and the wealthy alike, because there is food in the land.

Deuteronomy 12 and 14 are two of the most exciting chapters in the Bible when it comes to the tithe. Here tithing is not a drudgery. It's not a civic duty and it's not a simple 'return unto God what is His already.' No, it's a celebration! God has done it again! He has provided a bounty of food for an entire nation.

According to the Law of Moses, there was a particular place where the Israelites were to take their tithes and their sacrifices, their burnt-offerings and heave-offerings, and even that which they vowed to the Lord. They were not, like the heathen nations which they destroyed and displaced, allowed to bring their gifts to God to every high place and spreading tree.[17] The pagans worshiped gods of nature. But the Israelites worshiped the Most High God, possessor of heaven and earth.

God chose a place for his Name and a city for his throne; Jerusalem.[18] And no matter where you lived in the nation of Israel, God's house was the only appropriate place to bring tithes, offerings, and sacrifices.

"And there you shall eat before the Lord your God, and you shall rejoice, you and your households, in all you undertake, in which the Lord your God has blessed you." (Deut. 12:7)

The celebration was because God had blessed the works of your hands. If you've ever farmed or gardened or raised livestock, you know that all your hard work can be brought to nothing for all kinds of reasons beyond your control. But when the nation Israel covenanted with God

---

[17] Deut. 12:2-6

[18] At the time the law was given, God had not yet told the Israelites Jerusalem was where his temple would be built. But he did indicate to them that he himself would choose the place for his Name.

and took up residence in the land of milk and honey, God made a promise.

Take a look in Deuteronomy chapter 11, verse 8, as God starts to build up toward chapter 12. First, He tells them the difference between where they came from and where they are going. (All emphasis is mine.)

> **8** "You shall therefore keep the whole commandment that I command you today, that you may be strong, and go in and take possession of the land that you are going over to possess,
>
> **9** and that you may live long in the land that the Lord swore to your fathers to give to them and to their offspring, a land flowing with milk and honey.
>
> **10** "For the land that you are entering to take possession of it is not like the land of Egypt, from which you have come, where you sowed your seed and irrigated it, like a garden of vegetables.
>
> **11** "But the land you are going over to possess is a land of hills and valleys, *which drinks water by the rains from heaven, 12) a land that the Lord your God cares for. The eyes of the Lord your God are always upon it, from the beginning of the year to the end of the year."*

Wow! Unlike the Egyptians who had built vast irrigation systems to water their crops from the Nile, the Israelites were going to live in a land that God himself took special care of. The stipulation was as follows:

> **13** "And if you will indeed obey my commandments that I command you today, to love the Lord your God, and to serve him with all your heart and with all your soul,
>
> **14** *he will give the rain for your land in its season, the early rain and the later rain, that you may gather in your grain and your wine and your oil.*

15 "And he will give grass in your fields for your livestock, and you shall eat and be full."

When we get to chapters 12 and 14, we see the people celebrating as God does just that, year after year. The tithe from the increase from the land, including the livestock which ate the grass which the land provided, was a part of that celebration.

The people were told that they, along with their families, servants, and the Levites from their towns, were to eat the tithe! And the reason they ate was because they were rejoicing before the Lord regarding how what they had put their hand to that year had prospered. What's more, since they were eating before the Lord, or in His presence, not only had they brought their tithe-gift, but the Lord generously shared it with all.

I had not known that the people who tithed were expected to themselves personally enjoy, during this time of celebration, a portion of what they brought in. What's more, they were to choose for their meal whatever their hearts desired. Did they want meat? The finest steak or the most tender lamb? They were welcome to it. Whatever their soul longed to eat, they could have it.[19] What about foods that weren't clean according to the law? Based on Deut. 12:22 it seems they could enjoy that also. The only thing they were to abstain from was eating blood.

When I look at Deut. 14:22-29 I see a little more detail. Some people lived quite some distance from the place where God chose to put His Name, and it would have been a burden to transport grains or drive livestock so far. They were given the option to sell their tithes in their hometown, travel to the festival, then use the money to... Well, I'll let the Bible itself tell you.

24 "And if the way is too long for you, so that you are not able to carry the tithe, when the Lord your God blesses you, because the place is too far from you, which the Lord your God chooses, to set his name there,

---

[19] Deut. 12:20-21

25 "then you shall turn it into money and bind up the money in your hand and go to the place that the Lord your God chooses **26** and spend the money for whatever you desire - oxen or sheep or wine or strong drink, whatever your appetite craves. And you shall eat there before the Lord your God and rejoice, you and your household."

Again, they are reminded to remember those who do not tithe: the Levite, the stranger, the fatherless and the widows who dwell where they live. Their tithe doesn't just sit in the storehouses all year long to be doled out as needed. These also are to come and celebrate, and to eat and be satisfied.

One thing I notice is that the tithe offering is entirely agricultural in nature. Even when circumstances caused them to change their tithe into money, upon reaching their destination they must change it back to food and drink before celebrating. The wonderful thing is they can use the money to buy something different if they wish.

Can you imagine anything that would make you feel more generous than to go up to Jerusalem with the priests of God, the stranger, and the needy of your hometown, and then happily feed them whatever their hearts' desire? I suspect that would really tie a community together with compassion over the course of the year.

There is much more on tithing in the books of the law, but I'd like to look at just one more passage. The very last chapter of Leviticus is a listing of the many ways one might give to the Lord. It starts with a valuation of persons who make a vow to the Lord and continues on till it discusses the tithe.

What is interesting to me is this, the tithe is only one method of many ways to give to the Lord. One could sanctify their house to be holy to the Lord. One could also sanctify part of their field. In both cases, the person could, if they desired, redeem the property by adding 20% to the valuation of it. At that point, it returns to their hands and remains in the family inheritance.

One could also devote things to the Lord. Things that have been devoted are considered most holy to the Lord and cannot be redeemed. The tithe, though, (Lev. 27:30-33) is also holy to the Lord, but (with the exception discussed in vs. 32-33) a man has the right of redemption.

This chapter particularly brings two questions to my mind. First, I was surprised that arrangements could be made for someone to redeem their tithe. Obviously, this cannot be done with the money. Paying $120 to get $100 in cash back doesn't make sense. But the original concept of tithing has never been a matter of money. Paying (as a modern example) $120 to get back a sheep valued at $100 makes a little more sense. A quality sheep has more purposes for the owner than money sitting in a vault somewhere does.

My second question is to wonder why, with the four options of vows, sanctification, devoting and tithing, did we somehow get stuck just on the tithe option? Surely if we are expected to tithe, we would equally be expected to vow or devote or sanctify things to the Lord.

As with all studies, when something puzzles me, I put it on the backburner and pray for an answer later on. In the meantime, since Malachi 3:8-11 is an often quoted argument for tithing, I feel it is important to go there next.

About Robbing God

One thing most believers have in common is we all want to do right by God. So when we are accused of robbing God, we sit up and take notice. The relevant passage involves four verses in Malachi, chapter three. And I am focused on these four verses because, when they are quoted, the verses prior to and after are rarely included.

> 8 "Will a man rob God? Yet you are robbing me. But you say, 'How have we robbed you?' In your tithes and contributions.

9 You are cursed with a curse, for you are robbing me, the whole nation of you.

10 "Bring the full tithe into the storehouse, that there may be food in my house. And thereby put me to the test, says the Lord of hosts, if I will not open the windows of heaven for you and pour down for you a blessing until there is no more need.

11 "I will rebuke the devourer for you, so that it will not destroy the fruits of your soil, and your vine in the field shall not fail to bear, says the Lord of hosts."

When these verses are taught as a reason to tithe, they are normally interpreted to mean if we don't tithe, we are robbing God of what is rightfully his and our finances are cursed as a result. However if we tithe the full amount then God will reward us with abundant material blessings in this life.

The first thing I notice is I have to deal with the end of verse 10. Then I will need to find out the context because I really feel as if I have been dropped into the middle of a discussion.

My problem with verse 10 is the last phrase says "pour down for you a blessing until there is no more need." It makes me curious about the accuracy of the translation.

I tend to like the English Standard Version because "The ESV is an 'essentially literal' translation that seeks as far as possible to capture the precise wording of the original text and the personal style of each Bible writer."[20] However the King James Version, which I also enjoy, reads "... and pour you out a blessing, that there shall not be room enough to receive it." This gives an entirely different understanding, so I feel the need to try and determine which translation is closest to the original meaning.

[20] English Standard Bible, Preface, Translation Philosophy, copyright 2005, Crossway Bibles, Good News Publishers.

Young's Literal Translation, which can be even more literal than the ESV, says, "Bring in all the tithe unto the treasure-house, And there is food in My house; When ye have tried Me, now, with this, Said Jehovah of Hosts, Do not I open to you the windows of heaven? Yea, I have emptied on you a blessing till there is no space."[21]

Keeping these various translations in mind, I move on. I realize that I will need to understand the book of Malachi in order to figure out the context. Fortunately, Malachi is a relatively short book as the Bible goes. A mere four chapters.

Malachi was written about the time of Nehemiah, meaning the Temple had been rebuilt after the Babylonian Exile, and worship had been re-established. Malachi's purpose was to rebuke both the people and the priests for their disregard of the law and to remind them of God's faithfulness and love for them. Nehemiah took them to task for many of the same problems.

The people were using blemished animals to fulfill their vows. The priests who were to serve God were instead dishonoring the Name of the Lord by offering blind, lame, and sick animals to God, presumably keeping the better ones for themselves. Remember, in regard to tithes, every tenth animal that went under the shepherd's rod went to the Lord. The person bringing the animals weren't allowed to make substitutions, either a bad one for a better one or a good one for a bad one.

Another problem was that the men of Israel were marrying heathen women, sometimes even divorcing virtuous Hebrew wives in order to do so. The priesthood was complicit by allowing these divorces to take place. They also showed partiality rather than justice when it came to the law. God said that He cursed their blessings because of this.[22]

Aside from the intermarriages with women who followed false gods, the people were accused of sorcery, adultery, and bearing false

---

21

https://www.biblegateway.com/passage/?search=Malachi+3%3A10&version=YLT

[22] Mal. 2:1-2

witness. God was also against those who oppressed the hired worker in his wages, the widow, the fatherless, and the stranger.[23] The last three, recall, were the normal recipients of tithes.

Immediately following this verse the Lord points out that He is faithful. "I change not." From the time Israel was established, they kept turning away from God's ordinances. But because God does not change, He remained faithful and so did not destroy them. He calls them to repent and return to Him. But during Malachi's time they couldn't seem to figure out what the problem is. So God spells it out.

"Remember the tithes and offerings by which the widow, the fatherless and the stranger are fed? You're not bringing it in. Therefore, there is no meat in my house with which to feed the neediest of my people.[24] Who do you think you are, robbing God?"

They had an agreement. God would send the early rains and the latter rains in their season. He would provide the rain for their crops and to grow the grass for their herds. He would feed them all! And they would bring in their tithes in celebration and in gratitude.

> **13** "And if you will indeed obey my commandments that I command you today, to love the Lord your God, and to serve him with all your heart and with all your soul,
>
> **14** he will give the rain for your land in its season, the early rain and the later rain, that you may gather in your grain and your wine and your oil.
>
> **15** And he will give grass in your fields for your livestock, and you shall eat and be full."[25]

Think about it. Not only are they defrauding the laborer of his wages, but they are withholding that which God used to feed the needy.

---

[23] Mal. 3:5
[24] Mal. 3:8-10 (personal paraphrase)
[25] Deut. 11:13-15

There was no sharing from the fields with the poor as they all ate at God's table. It seems the poor were being robbed from both directions.

I noticed God didn't mention the priests were suffering lack from the giving of an incomplete tithe. Remember the Levites and the priests were also to be fed from the tithes, but as we saw, the priests were managing to get theirs, and giving God the leftovers.

The problem was not just the quality of the tithes themselves. Rather the shortage of tithes reflected the people's attitudes. They were selfish and hard-hearted. They kept the best for themselves and had no regard for their fellow citizens who lacked the basic necessities of life. And because of this attitude toward those God cared about, God withheld the blessings of his provision and let the curse overtake them.

Amos, chapter 4 shows a similar situation. Right in the first verse God is rebuking the women of Samaria for oppressing the poor and crushing the needy while they loll about in luxury, drinking wine with their husbands. In this case, the people *did* bring their tithes and sacrifices to the Lord. It was their attitudes toward the needy that the Lord punished them for.

He withheld rain from their crops when they were still three months away from the harvest. Remember, they didn't have irrigation systems like the Egyptians did. They were dependent upon God's favor and the rain he sent. What rain he did allow was erratic. It would rain on one field, but not on another. And he would allow pestilence and insects to devour their crops.

"I struck you with blight and mildew; your many gardens and your vineyards, your fig trees and your olive trees the locust devoured, yet you did not return to me," declares the Lord.[26]

Humanity's relationship with God has always been about more than just bringing offerings and going through religious rituals. It has also been about our relationships with each other. Although Amos shows the

---

[26] Amos 4:5

44

people bringing all kinds of offerings before God, their offerings were rejected because of injustice in the land.

So now when we look at Malachi 3:10-12, we understand what the Lord means when he says they need to bring the whole tithe so that there might be meat in his house. And His promise to open the windows of heaven means what it has always meant: rain! See Genesis 7:11, 8:2 and the account of the flood.

This seems to mean that the blessing he pours out of which it says "until there is no more need," refers to the annual blessing of an abundance of food for everyone. With God watching over the land of Israel, the insects which devour the crops are rebuked, and the fruit is not cast from the vine prior to the harvest.

Mal. 3:12 emphasizes that God's blessing on the land is what sustains his people. "Then all nations will call you blessed, for you will be a *land of delight*, says the Lord of hosts."[27]

Now, every Israeli land and herd owning citizen wasn't at fault. The end of Chapter 3 and all of Chapter 4 indicates that God is quite able to differentiate between the righteous and the wicked. Perhaps when He urged them to "bring the full tithe into the storehouse," he wasn't implying that everyone was skimping on what they owed. We tend to think this verse points to individual sin. Rather, it was the cumulative tithe received from everyone in the nation who worked the fields or herded flock that made it possible for there to be "no more need."

With this fuller understanding of the ways and purposes of tithing as practiced in the Old Testament, I now wonder how far we wandered so far afield from its origins. Has there been a logical progression from the law of Moses as depicted in Deuteronomy to the present day version? At what point did it begin to change and why?

---

[27] Emphasis mine

Chapter Four

The Historic Tithe

Modern Tithing Roots - Traditional

The church, meaning the worldwide assembly of the followers of Jesus Christ, began at Pentecost. While we do have Biblical evidence on the activities of this early church, to follow the history of tithing up to the present day I needed to find other historical documents.

The church, originally identified as a Jewish sect called the Way,[28] over the next few centuries became the catholic (meaning 'universal') church. This evolved into the Roman Catholic Church as it became a more formal and state-sanctioned organization, and then the church splintered into a variety of denominations with different beliefs regarding the interpretation of certain scriptures.

---

[28] Acts 22:4

I decided to start by looking into the history of tithing in the Catholic Church, whose records go back the furthest. I was rather surprised to find that the modern day Catholic Church also seems to be confused about whether tithing is a valid doctrine. The 'Catholic Answers' website states that, while all adults who are able should support the church by giving, the church doesn't specify a particular amount.[29] This seems to be the official position.

However, their websites are as inundated as Protestant ones are with the query, "Are we supposed to tithe?" Despite the official position, there are parishes which do encourage tithing. And at least one instance where there was a call to "withhold the tithe from dioceses and parishes whose clergy do not adhere to the Catholic faith." Which indicates that, somewhere, there is a tithe being given that could be withheld.

To learn a bit about the historical aspects of the tithe, I looked at the work of Russell Earl Kelly, Ph.D. for his very thorough research regarding all aspects of the subject. While there never seems to have been 100% agreement within the church as to whether tithing is a valid teaching, there were some landmarks in history which I will list here.

To put it bluntly, the early church did not tithe. As I will discuss in a later chapter, they were more dependent upon freewill offerings, the purpose of which was not to support the administration of the church itself. While tithing was suggested once or twice around 300-400 A.D., nothing came of it. So my timeline begins somewhat later. Remember that in the beginning, there was only one church. And so the term Church refers to what we now think of as the Roman Catholic Church. Other denominations did not spring up until later.

Some key historical events regarding tithing are as follows.

567 A.D. - At the Council of Tours, the Church first attempts to enforce tithing, rather than continue to let it be voluntary.

---

[29] *Catholic Answers.* http://www.catholic.com/quickquestions/what-is-the-churchs-position-on-tithing

584 A.D. - At the Council of Macon, believers were ordered to pay tithes with the threat of excommunication towards those who refused. In these early days, tithes appeared to be food goods and possibly land.

785 A.D. - Charlemagne promulgated a decree and signed the compulsory payment of tithes into civil law.

906 A.D. - "King Edgar legally enforced food tithing in England." "All citizens, including Jews, were required to tithe to the Roman Catholic Church. A typical peasant was giving the first tithe of his land to his secular ruler or landlord (which was often the church) and a second tenth to the church outright."[30]

1524 A.D. - Otto Brumfels, a German theologian and botanist, proclaims that the New Testament church does not teach tithing.

1789 A.D. - France abolishes tithes.

1836-1850 - Tithing is mostly abolished in England.

While the United States churches had various ways of giving designed to support themselves, since the federal government was prohibited by the first amendment from either establishing a state religion or exercising any authority over matters of religion, tithing was never a federal requirement for U.S. citizens.

The Bill of Rights, Amendment I reads - "Congress shall make no law respecting an establishment of religion, or prohibiting the free exercise thereof..."[31]

Instead, American churches depended on freewill offerings, pew rentals, local taxes and the like.

The turning point seemed to be J.W. Pratt's 1873 essay, "Will A Man Rob God?" This quickly became a favorite sermon topic and continues so to this day. Since the teaching of a tithe doctrine in the U.S.

---

[30] www.tithing-russkelly.com/id15.html
[31] Bill of Rights, Passed by Congress Sept 25, 1789, Ratified Dec. 15, 1791.

is well over a century old, I can see how modern day Christians can believe it is a long held truth and set in stone. After all, we've heard it all our lives as did our parents and grandparents.

It wasn't until the mid-1900s that the concept of tithing as well as other forms of giving transformed into what is now known as the prosperity gospel. The key figure here was Oral Roberts.

Modern Tithing Roots - Prosperity

Oral Roberts' ministry was considered the beginning of the modern prosperity or seed-faith gospel. His ministry was largely considered that of a healing ministry. Roberts also included messages of positivity.

According to beliefnet.com, "Roberts had one life message, summed up in a variety of sayings as he preached over the years: "Something good is going to happen to you." "God is a good God." "All things are possible." "Expect a miracle."[32] These are the messages I was exposed to while at college in the early 1980s and the songs we sang as a choir reinforced these beliefs.

Oral Roberts' teachings influenced several generations of modern day ministers including three prominent preachers who I consider the 1st generation of prosperity ministers: Kenneth Hagin (ORU[33] graduate), Kenneth Copeland (ORU attendee), and Fred Price (honorary Doctorate of Divinity from ORU). Today we have what I consider 2nd generation ministers such as Ted Haggard and Joel Osteen, those who appeared to be either influenced by the 1st generation ministers or attended ORU themselves.

Mr. Roberts himself started out as a lay minister with a Pentecostal background, then attended Oklahoma Baptist College for

---

[32] http://www.beliefnet.com/faiths/christianity/protestant/2009/the-legacy-of-oral-roberts.aspx#vPsUFXRd11VUsKT5.99
[33] Oral Roberts University

additional training. This is a common path for those who feel they have been called to preach.

Chief among his ORU teachings was the Seed-Faith message, a gospel that proclaimed when you "sowed a financial seed" into God's work God would give you a financial blessing in return. This financial blessing could be monetary in nature or consist of high-quality material goods.

Most historians agree that Oral Roberts was influenced by a book called "Think and Grow Rich" by Napolean Hill. This book is still available and is considered the "granddaddy of all motivational literature."

An example of Mr. Hill's type of thinking is the following quote from his book: "There is a difference between WISHING for a thing and being READY to receive it. No one is ready for a thing, until he believes he can acquire it. The state of mind must be BELIEF, not mere hope or wish. Open-mindedness is essential for belief."

In other words, from him, we get the idea that if we approach something with enough belief then we can receive or acquire it. This eventually developed into the pseudo-Christian concept that I learned while in school: if the mind can conceive it, then you can achieve it. Name it and claim it.

There is no evidence that Napolean Hill was ever a Christian and he did not set out to espouse Christian principles. His books were based on his study of the great business minds of his time, particularly the principles for success of Andrew Carnegie, a steel magnate. His purpose was to urge people towards business success.

Such teachings, filtered through scriptures such as III John 1:2 - "Beloved, I wish above all things that thou mayest prosper and be in health, even as thy soul prospereth,"[34] were interpreted as God's desire for us to be financially prosperous while on this earth.

---

[34] Holy Bible, KJV

I wondered if there was a bit of a quirk in translation there. The King James Version was the most popular, indeed almost the only, translation used in the United States at the time that this particular verse caught Oral Roberts' eye and imagination. The Young's Literal translation also uses the word 'prosper,' and my interlinear Greek New Testament[35] identifies the same word when translated directly from the Greek language.

The problem, then, was determining how the word 'prosper' was defined? Some Bible translations define it in a general rather than financial way, such as the English Standard Version:

"Beloved, I pray that all may go well with you and that you may be in good health, as it goes well with your soul." (ESV)

Current dictionaries indicate both a modern definition ("to be successful or fortunate, especially in financial respects") and an archaic definition which was likely in use at the time the KJV was written, where "to make fortunate" meant more along the lines of "to make happy."

So it seemed the idea that God's plan is to make all believers wealthy is likely based on a more modern mindset of what the word 'prosper' means. Once that idea takes hold, it then becomes easy to locate other scriptures which agree with your interpretation. (You can do this with almost any personal philosophy or theological interpretation you have your mind set on. As an example, slavery in the United States was once justified using scriptures from the Bible.)

The result, as could be expected, was the evolution of a 'prosperity gospel.' As one pastor pointed out, the gospel, or good news, for poor people is you don't have to be poor anymore. This sort of viewpoint alone would make a prosperity gospel popular.

Understanding this gaves me a good idea how we got to the point we are now at. Since there is a disparity between present-day

---

[35] An interlinear translation is a good way for a Bible student to get at the original Greek word without needing to learn to read in the original language.

traditional teachings and prosperity teachings, yet the tithe is evident in both, I wanted to look at them next.

Chapter Five

Traditional and Prosperity Teachings

I had not known that all the denominational branches of Christianity do not teach tithing as a doctrine. What I had assumed to be a universal teaching was clearly not. In fact, churches which instruct believers to tithe are in the minority.

Modern churches which do teach the doctrine of tithing tend to fall into one of two broad categories: traditional teachings and prosperity teachings.

Traditional teachings hold sway in mainline churches and are primarily what you will hear in most, but not all, Catholic and Protestant Christian churches. Prosperity teachings diverge from those roots in their core beliefs about money and the modern Christian, and what the expected response from God for our giving is.

I have been trained under both teachings. The churches I grew up in taught that 10% of your income was to go to the church. I remember friends of mine, a brother and sister, received $10 every week as an allowance, with the stipulation that $1 was to go into the offering. Since I didn't receive an allowance and rarely had any money to handle, the issue actually never came up for myself until I attended college.

When I started attending East Carolina University in the late 1970s, it was the first time I had enough money that it required management. It was also the first time I'd heard teachings outside the beliefs of the churches I grew up with. TV preachers like Frederick K. Price and Kenneth Copeland were rising stars in televangelism and were prominent sources of inspiration at the Fountain of Life Christian Fellowship, a black student ministry I joined. This period of my life was also my first exposure to lengthy sermons on the importance of tithes and offerings.

In 1980, we discovered Faith and Victory Church, a local storefront church just started by Pastor John Zabawski and his wife Deborah. To my delight, they didn't feed their fledgling congregation spiritual milk; meaning the basic tenets of the gospel. They just dove in deep into some challenging material and assumed you'd keep up. The teaching was so in-depth that it excited the college students from the Fellowship, and we helped swell their membership. Some of them are there to this day.

I honestly don't remember if he taught much on tithing. Pastor Zabawski's sermons and Bible study classes covered a wide range of biblical topics, and no one particular subject was emphasized over the others. In hindsight, his teachings and my own church background probably balanced out the influence of nationally popular teachers like Copeland and Price, whom I heard speak only occasionally.

Traditional teachings on tithing focus on the following points.

1- 10% of one's earned income is to be given to the church.

2- Both a tithe and a separate offering are to be given.

3- Tithes and offerings are a matter of giving back to God out of what he has blessed you with. In a sense, because everything belongs to Him, you are returning to God what is already his.

4- Tithes and offerings are monetary. (This was more an assumption than a teaching, based on point number one.)

5- Tithes and offerings are intended to support the church and its ministries.

The traditional-style churches I am accustomed to may also include other types of offerings which don't necessarily relate back to the Law of Moses:

1- Love Offerings – These are usually intended to be given to a guest preacher to express gratitude for their visit and perhaps help cover traveling expenses. They may also be asked for a family which has experienced some sort of sudden crisis. Love offerings are asked for on an intermittent basis.

2- Building Fund Offerings – These are specifically for the maintenance and possible expansion of the church structure. Many churches didn't collect a separate offering for this, they simply had it as an option on the tithing envelope you put your money in.

3- Missions Offerings – Designated for spreading the gospel and assisting others outside of the church. As a frequent member of a Missionary Baptist churches, I noted these funds were also used in visitation of the membership's sick and shut-in.

4- Sunday School Offerings – These are taken only during the pre-worship service educational classes on Sunday and are normally intended to provision Sunday School classes with teaching materials and student books.

5- Sacrificial Offerings – This is not typically considered a separate offering in a church with traditional teaching. But this term is now often heard as a prelude to asking for an offering, usually for a special purpose; perhaps a Love Offering or a particular building fund need. The request is that you give sacrificially, meaning beyond your normal offering, even beyond your fiscal ability, in order to meet a need. You sacrifice something in order to give.

One key difference between traditional and prosperity teachings is the emphasis on the importance of the tithe. Traditional churches include tithing as just one of many important lessons a believer must learn. Other subjects such as the need for forgiveness, salvation, and faithfulness are given equal emphasis. Tithing is encouraged and perhaps expected but rarely demanded of their membership. Prosperity ministry churches tend to present the need to give tithes and offerings as the most important lesson, often making it the subject of every sermon.

Prosperity teachings go by a number of names. For example, they are also referred to as Word of Faith or Seed-Faith Teachings. When it comes to tithing, the focus is on the following teaching points:

1- A tithe is 10% of one's gross earned income. (Some, but not all, expand their definition of income to include other sources for the money you may receive.)

2- Both a tithe and a separate offering are to be given, with the tithe given first.

3- God commands us to tithe. Not tithing is an act of disobedience.

4- There are Spiritual Laws that govern tithing. Following these laws will result in financial growth. Not following these laws, even inadvertently, will result in financial stagnation or poverty.

5- God cannot or will not act on our behalf financially if we are not obedient to his command to tithe. He acts within the Spiritual Laws he himself has established. Therefore, we must make the first move in giving as a demonstration of our faith.

6- Sacrificial offerings are strongly encouraged as an act of faith and as a means of turning your financial situation around.

The prosperity teachings generally don't identify as many types of offerings as traditional churches. Instead, they lean toward the following, any of which can be placed in the offering plate together:

1- The Tithe – Defined as 10% of what God has given you.

2- The Offering – Anything that you give after you have given your tithe.

3- The Seed-Offering – A special, often sacrificial offering. This is likened to sowing a seed into the ground. A subsequent financial harvest in return is to be expected when you give this.

As I moved from place to place, it became evident over time that non-traditional teachings regarding the tithe were slowly being absorbed into mainstream churches. Because I was a more or less lifelong church attendee, how the church services and sermons changed over the years became very evident to me. Plus, because I moved so often, I still attended the occasional church that was not linked to my original denomination, such as Pentecostal, Episcopalian, and Church of God in Christ, so I could see the differences.

I can tell you from experience, in some of the churches the pressure to give as much as you can quickly became enormous. Let's go back to Tithe-Guilt for a minute. These are additional guilt-inducing giving opportunities I have faced.

1- **The challenge of multiple offerings.** At one church, my typical week found me faced with five separate offering plates. They included the Sunday School offering (if you have children, you need to give them money for each of their class offerings, too), Sunday Morning Worship Service (if they held it down to one offering and didn't collect a special offering), Sunday Evening Worship Service, Wednesday Night Bible Study, and the Friday Joy Night Service.

(To this day, I still don't understand why an offering would be taken up at something like Bible Study since that is not a worship service. But that's my personal beef. Weekly Prayer Meetings did not include an offering opportunity.)

For someone who received a paycheck once every two weeks, I found myself with two choices. I could split up what was designated for the offering plate so that I could be seen to give into each offering. Or I could give the tithe all at one shot the first chance I got, then dribble dollars into the remaining offerings over the next two weeks.

2- **The pre-offering mini-sermon.** This can be as short as a few sentences reminding us we are expected to give both tithes and offerings. However, they can go on for much longer. The longest I ever endured was weekly half-hour exhortations prior to the Sunday worship service offering.

If you were tithing that day, it allowed you to feel a little self-righteous about it, though eventually even you were ready to move on to the rest of the service. If you weren't tithing you were going to squirm. But you had thirty minutes to decide whether you were actually capable of giving more than your original intention. Most traditionally based churches, including my current one, do not do the pre-offering pep talk.

3- **The "Robbing God" accusations.** From what I know of my fellow Christians, no true believer wants to rob the God they love. If you just could not get your tithe together, but you wanted to, this one really nips at your conscience.

4- **The "You're under a curse" explanation.** This is linked with the "Robbing God" one and is grounded in Malachi 3:8-11. The explanation is it is tithing which lifts the curse that is currently keeping you poor.

The subtext is: it's your own fault you don't have enough money. If you really had the faith to give more generously to your church and didn't forget the tithe, God would practically flood your life with money.

5- **Public shaming.** This is extreme and I am grateful that even most prosperity ministries don't stoop to this. Usually, it is a reverse psychology method of shaming. The person who didn't give as expected is not actually pointed out, but since those who did are lifted up as examples, those who do not become obvious.

My daughter attended a church which did this. Several times a year they had "Super Sundays," which were services devoted to giving sacrificially both to help the growing (storefront) church and to plant a seed for your own needs. The members were asked to sow a seed into the ministry by giving $1,000 or $5,000 or $10,000. Those who managed this were brought up to the front of the church, the amount they had given was announced, and they were praised for their faith and faithfulness. Those who could not or would not give as requested remained quite obviously in their seats.

It was this sort of embarrassing situation that impelled my daughter to start studying tithing independently. She subsequently learned the importance of identifying scriptural context when she read her Bible. And eventually dug in her heels on such extreme giving.

Since she was on the church staff, they had decided she was a spiritual leader (she wasn't, she was a graphic designer with no ministerial background) and so was required to tithe on the minuscule paycheck they gave her, which was less than half of what people with her skills generally earned. She and the church eventually had to part ways.

6- **The Beyond the Grave Plea.** I'm actually starting to see these advertisements in magazines. I have not noticed a church yet that mentions it. Not even the prosperity ministries. But it's probably coming. The idea is to do estate planning so that, when you're gone to be with the Lord, instead of leaving everything to your families, you can continue to promote the mission of the church.

7- **The True Testimony Pressure Test.** These are the deeply moving stories of those who gave sacrificially and almost immediately received a substantial blessing from God. The subtext is: God does this sort of thing all the time. This should be your testimony. You need to demonstrate more faith by giving more.

8- **Americans are selfish and spoiled accusations.** There are two versions of this. The first compares the annual incomes of American citizens with the incomes of citizens from more impoverished nations. "We have televisions and microwaves and cell phones in nearly every home. It is evident that are a nation of great wealth compared to other nations."

This is true if you're only matching dollar to dollar across the globe. But when you factor in the local cost of living and its real life effect on families, you may get a different picture. Yes, we make far more than $40 a month. But we cannot fathom living in a country where $40 a month will actually provide food and shelter for a family of four, even if it's just rice and beans. In the United States, a family of four living on $2,628 a month is considered poverty level for good reason, especially if they live in a large city.

The other version of this accusation implies that if we just eliminate our weekly pizza delivery or our daily latte we could free up plenty of money for the kingdom of God. We can't possibly presume to know the circumstances of other believers. That nice home they live in may be teetering on the edge of foreclosure. A surfeit of bills may mean a particular family hasn't had the pleasure of eating out for over a year. A request for $20 from each family to help the church out may be a request for their grocery money.

9- **The Real Faith Would Make It Happen pressure.** This is pressure I put on myself. A few moments with my paycheck and a calculator tells me that I can't do it all. Yet either I continued to try because I thought it was a test of my faith, or I ducked my perceived spiritual obligations in order to buy food. Or to replace somebody's shoes. And failed the test.

According to my 'Real Faith Would Make It Happen' beliefs if I had just given God his money, He would have shortly given it back to me with compound interest, thus proving His word and allowing me to buy the food we needed.

This compound interest thing was based on the teaching that I would receive a twenty-fold, sometimes a hundredfold, return for my investment into the spiritual kingdom of God. This teaching is based on Matt. 13:23 where seed cast on good soil yields a hundredfold, or sixty, or thirtyfold return. This is an outgrowth of the Seed-Faith teachings. When the passage is taken in context, it becomes obvious that Jesus isn't talking about money. But of course, I didn't know that then.

Based on my personal history with God, I eventually realized this lavish return of my funds probably wasn't going to happen. I tested it and had been doing so for over two decades, as God apparently told me to do in Malachi. And... nothing. Yeah, I'm probably doing something wrong, I told myself. I'm probably lacking in sufficient faith. It took years before I understood that God simply doesn't work that way.

In other words, if the hundredfold return is a Spiritual Law, then it should work for everyone every time. That's what laws do. If it only works some of the time then that implies some capriciousness on God's part or some frisky doings in your legal system. And frankly, I stand by my belief that God is a god that doesn't change, but rather is eternally faithful to His word.

"Let God be true though everyone were a liar..."[36]

This morning I watched a well-known preacher from "Campmeeting Inspiration Ministries." Incidentally, this minister's doctorate is an honorary degree in theology from the non-accredited International Seminary in Florida. My daughter's former pastor and his wife also possessed honorary degrees in theology. While I don't believe you have to be a theologian in order to preach the gospel, if you state you do have a doctorate in theology, then I expect you to have had the actual training.

---

[36] Rom. 3:4

I hadn't listened closely to this type of teaching since my college days, and I wanted to see how things might have changed. Campmeeting Inspiration Ministries is what I think of as hardcore prosperity teaching. Softcore prosperity teaching is more of a feel-good gospel with the benefits of tithing thrown in on a regular basis.

The following comes from my notes. The preacher was preaching on "The Law of the Seed," part of a series on the 7 Laws. According to him, God said, "When I talk to you about a seed, I have a harvest on my mind. Nothing leaves heaven until something leaves earth. The seed that leaves your hand will never leave your life. It goes into your future where it will multiply."

This was followed shortly by a personal testimony where the preacher was once poor but obediently sowed a $1,000 seed anyway. The next day a man gave him a rare automobile because God told him to. The following day someone bought a fan for his ministry because God told them to give it to this preacher. (I presume it was an expensive piece of equipment for a building and not a box fan. But he didn't explain.) Then the following day he received a check for $10,000 because God told someone to give that to him. He says, "I broke the back of poverty with a thousand dollar seed." I was amazed that he took credit for what was presumably God's work.

Then he started to prophesy, saying that God was putting into his spirit a vision of 300 people and a 17-minute window. He was going to pray, he said, and when he stopped praying there was going to be a 17-minute window of time where God was planning to bless the first 300 people who planted a $1,000 seed into this particular ministry.

These 300 people would receive 'the most glorious favor you've ever had' over the next 90 days. God would multiply their seed. In other words, based on the amount of money they gave the ministry, the minimum acceptable "seed" apparently being $1,000, God would multiply that amount and return it to them.

What's more, according to this preacher, God was promising that every unsaved person in the families of these 300 would become saved. I could see how that would strike the hearts of every mother out there praying for her children. There was also something about Christians owning seven houses, all mortgage free, but I couldn't quite figure out what was going on there.

As soon as he finished praying the psychological pressure was on. And it was extreme! Having myself once been susceptible to this style of creative theology, I could only feel sorry for the panic-stricken Christians lunging for their phones.

To discourage listeners from thinking it over, discussing it with their spouse or, heaven forbid, even praying about it, he let them know that "Delayed obedience is always disobedience!" "Delayed obedience is rebellion!" "Do it quickly!   Do it right now!" He didn't want them to hesitate and he certainly didn't want them to give them a chance to think. With the clock ticking down and the possibility of not getting through the phone lines in time, they just might miss this unexpected outpouring from God.

When these teachings were addressed to Christians who were not yet familiar with the Scriptures for themselves, it was probably like shooting fish in a barrel. Although I hadn't been under a version of prosperity ministry quite this extreme, I was starting to understand where some of the Tithe-Guilt came from. Once you've been listening to sermons like this for months on end, you really don't have a lot of defenses left. With so many scriptures being quoted it all just sounds so logical and holy and right.

For those who perhaps couldn't immediately figure out where they could pull $1,000, he had suggestions. His first one was to use a credit card. I was in a church once that announced they would now take credit cards in order for their members to pay their tithes.

Having struggled with credit card debt for most of my life (hey, I told you I didn't handle money until I hit college) I was appalled. Christians who didn't have enough money on hand to pay a tithe were expected to borrow the money, then pay it back over time with interest to a credit card company? And since they weren't likely to have it paid back by the time more tithes were due ...

The preacher repeated the idea that they should sow this seed with a credit card several times. He said "You can't buy a miracle with a check. Or cash." Wow. I wanted to ask "Why not?" But of course, that gets into the whole argument of whether one could or should buy a miracle in the first place.

Another suggestion was to raid your savings or another bank account. Or use your mortgage money. (Don't worry about paying your mortgage or needing your savings, because obviously God was going to give it all back to you shortly.)

He then gave a testimony about a young couple who couldn't afford the $1,000 and so decided to borrow it in order to obediently plant that seed. Within 30 days, he claims they told him, God gave their church $100 million dollars. One. Hundred. Million. Dollars. I presume they themselves still owed $1,000 to whomever they borrowed it from.

He put a disclaimer at the end of this story by saying he didn't normally recommend borrowing the money. But by even telling the story he put the idea out there. Viewers were encouraged not to give up, but keep trying to get through. "Do it now! Find the money! It's important to do it now!"

My husband suggested that this was probably a recorded program, and I thought the hairstyles and clothes suggested sometime in the 1980s. But every time this program aired if you hadn't seen it before the prophecy would appear new. Most pre-recorded programs will have a little ribbon of words running along the bottom of the screen letting you know not to call in because this is over and done with. This one didn't. We presumed that so long as they had people standing by on the phones, the ministry could probably keep reaping income from that one broadcast for decades.

Possibly to cover their legal bases, a message popped up on the screen a couple of times during this giving telethon. But there were many other words on the screen to distract you. You would have had to be a fine-print reading fanatic like myself to even notice it. Each time it stayed on the screen only about 5 or 10 seconds and read as follows: "*Miracles are blessings from God and Inspiration Ministries does not guarantee miracles for everyone who gives.*" You bet!

Now this isn't to say that God does not do miracles. God *does* do miracles. I have been the grateful recipient of a few myself. He cannot, however, be manipulated into doing them on demand.

Give Me Your Tired, Your Poor, Your Huddled Masses Yearning to be Free

You're probably aware the above quote is inscribed on the base of the Statue of Liberty. What I discovered as I studied tithing this time around is this: the Christians most susceptible to such an extreme message are often poor, disadvantaged or financially desperate.

This teaching has a heavy emphasis on what the giver can expect to receive back. And those who struggle financially simultaneously have the most need of a sudden and massive influx of cash and are in the least position to give anything to anybody.

When I first heard it I was a college student with very limited resources. And both then and later I, too, tithed my heart out in hopes that God would help me out.

The Pew Research Center[37], in a mega-poll of nearly 35,000 people, learned that members of the Pentecostal denomination are the most likely to be taught that tithing is a necessity. It has, as I have noted, spread into many other denominations in some form or another. This group, however, is also described as having the lowest incomes and least education than any other Christian denomination. In other words, they really *really* need to keep the money that they do have and they do not

---

[37] www.pewforum.org

have enough theological background to challenge what's coming at them every time they sit down in the church pews.

This does not mean all Pentecostal churches teach the prosperity gospel, only that you should be aware when you listen to their teaching that they are very likely to. There are other denominations where these false doctrines have crept in and mingled with the truth.

Author and theologian Russell Earl Kelly, Ph.D., in one of his video tithing rebuttals, states that…

"The largest group in American society which approaches giving ten percent of their income to the church are ghetto-dwellers who faithfully sacrifice even disability and welfare checks in obedience to their pastors. Yet the greatest percent of them never escape poverty because they never get motivated to become educated and work long hard hours to get ahead in life. The vast majority of "tithers" never receive the "overflowing blessings and those who do are those who have persisted in other ways also. The blessings and curses of the Old Covenant ended at Calvary (Gal 3:13; Heb 8:3; 7:18)."[38]

I disagree with Dr. Kelly's belief that the primary reason poor people don't get ahead is a lack of motivation. Poverty is much more complex than that and can even be systemic in nature. But I do agree that these particular members of the body of Christ have an awesome faith in God!

With the idea that there are straightforward Spiritual Laws governing prosperity, and the tight focus on them being so thoroughly taught to their members, one would think such churches would gloat that they have the highest incomes of all Christians. Instead, the church itself does very well with ever increasing building programs (church buildings, universities, banks…) and lavish perks for their leadership. In a separate broadcast, the Campmeeting Inspiration Ministries preacher declared he could get your church out of debt.

---

[38] http://tithing-russkelly.com/id222.html

These churches wind up prospering in the modern sense on the backs of their lay members. But even though they give generously and often, the prospect of escaping debt or poverty continues to elude them.

Ezekiel 34 is a direct admonition to those shepherds that feed themselves instead of the flocks.[39] (In the interest of context I will tell you that Ezekiel 34 was written to the nation of Israel, not the as yet unestablished church. But as Peter also points out in the New Testament[40] that elders are expected to feed the flock of God, and not purely for the paycheck either, we can be assured that God hasn't changed his mind on this point even after the establishment of the body of Christ.)

Ezekiel tells us God is very much aware of what's going on and will not only judge the shepherds that are taking advantage of his sheep. He will also judge between the sheep that took advantage of the situation to fatten themselves up and those who were, in the end, simply trampled on.[41]

Obviously, there is nothing new under the sun. The Bible itself warns us that setting wealth as your goal, even as a goal with holy purposes, is to leave yourself open to all kinds of problems. Paul explained it to Timothy this way. "But those that desire to be rich fall into temptation, into a snare, into many senseless and harmful desires that plunge people into ruin and destruction."[42] It's a trap of which Christians should be wary.

Paul continues, "For the love of money is a root of all kinds of evils. It is through this craving that some have wandered away from the faith and pierced themselves with many pangs."

Surely not many of us as believers came to Christ because we wanted to get rich. We saw our spiritual needs and had matters of the heart on our minds. But when we wander away from the faith, I am glad that it is always open to us to repent and turn back to the right path.

---

[39] Ezek. 34:2-4
[40] I Pet. 5:1-3
[41] Ezek. 34:10, 15-22
[42] I Tim. 6:9-10 ESV

An International Teaching

I wondered if prosperity teachings were just an American phenomenon. I was willing to give it a little more credence if, like the Apostolic Creed, the majority of Christians understood it as part of the true gospel. The beliefs of a tiny portion of what is a 2,000-year ministry with millions of believers are not necessarily going to be wrong. But teachings (including my own) should be looked into more closely when they buck nearly everyone else's.

It turns out that the prosperity message is historically recent and started in the United States, primarily through Oral Roberts. But it is now huge in Nigeria with Bishop David Oyedepo's Canaanland, a church with the largest seating (50,000) in the world. Also, Pastor Enoch Adeboye's Redeemed Christian Church of God whose 40,000+ parishes have expanded beyond Nigeria and are now operative in over 186 countries in North America, Canada, and the United Kingdom.

Because of this, Word of Faith teachings and their take on tithing and giving can now be considered an international movement, even if these are not mainstream beliefs. However, even with such a wide ranging audience, the fact remains that the majority of Christians do not choose to follow these beliefs.

Chapter Six

A New Testament

There is little mention of tithing in the New Testament. As I searched, the first thing I wanted to know was whether Jesus had anything to say about my tithing. I mean, if anyone was going to get it right, it would be Jesus. Then I wanted to know what Paul and the other apostles who wrote the letters in the New Testament might have said.

I started off looking specifically for the word "tithe" or "tithing." But I would also look for any other mention of church expectations when it came to giving, even if the word tithe was not used. I also wanted to differentiate giving through tithing from simply giving.

My goal in determining my method of research was to put aside any preconceptions about what the verses mean, and so avoid reading any interpretation into the text that was not really there. As I said, it's relatively easy to interpret scripture to follow one's personal philosophy. Plus, if you have spent decades believing the Bible said such-and-such, it is more difficult than you can imagine to try and go back and pretend you'd never read any of it before and see it with a fresh eye.

The New Testament records just two instances of Jesus mentioning a tithe. In one case he was telling a parable about two men going up to the temple to pray. One was a Pharisee and the other a tax-collector.[43] According to Luke, Jesus "told this parable to some who trusted in themselves that they were righteous, and treat others with contempt."

The Pharisee of this parable prayed in this manner: "God, I thank you that I am not like the other men, extortioners, unjust, adulterers, or even like this tax collector. I fast twice a week; I give a tithe of all I get."

The tax collector's prayer was both simpler and more humble: "God, be merciful to me, a sinner!"

Jesus concludes this parable by saying, "I tell you, this man went down to his house justified, rather than the other. For everyone who exalts himself will be humbled, but the one who humbles himself will be exalted."

The purpose of the parable is to admonish God's people not to be self-righteous. The Pharisee, depicted as the proud one, reminded God of his obedience to the law, particularly in comparison to other men. In fact, he went above and beyond the requirements of the law in both his fasting and his tithing. Yet, in the end, his extraordinary, super-duper righteousness was not enough to justify him in the eyes of God.

While tithing is mentioned here, this is not a teaching *about* tithing. Rather this a teaching about sin and humility and God's grace. Tithing is simply used as a vehicle to expose the Pharisee's pride. At the most I can take away the fact that tithing was still a Jewish practice at the time of this teaching, and Jesus did not condemn it.

The second time Jesus mentioned tithing also had to do with the Pharisees. Both Matthew and Luke reported this teaching.[44] Looking at the contexts, it is not clear whether they are reporting the identical incident or two separate occasions. Both, however, are indictments

---

[43] Luke 18:9-14
[44] Matt. 23:23; Luke 11:42

against the Pharisees, calling them to account for their self-righteousness coupled with their hypocritical behavior.

> Matt. 23:23 – Woe unto you, scribes and Pharisees, hypocrites! For you tithe mint and dill and cumin, and have neglected the weightier matters of the law: justice and mercy and faithfulness. These you ought to have done, without neglecting the others.

> Luke 11:42 – But woe to you, Pharisees! For you tithe mint and rue and every herb, and neglect justice and the love of God. These you ought to have done, without neglecting the others.

In this case, Jesus mentioned food plants which are normally tithed from and argues that, while that was all well and good, the weightier matters of the law having to do with how you treat others and how you relate to God were left undone. All of the Law was to be obeyed, not just the showy bits.

Again, Jesus' focus was on their self-righteousness and their hypocritical behavior. While these passages may be used to argue that Jews ought to tithe, at least during the time period Jesus walked and taught among them, I can't reasonably relate it to the future church or myself without further evidence.

In regard to Jesus himself, neither he nor his parents would have tithed. When Mary and Joseph went to the Temple to present Mary's firstborn son before the Lord according to the Law, their offering was a pair of turtledoves or two young pigeons; the offering of the poor.[45]

As carpenters, neither Joseph nor Jesus qualified as landholders and did not raise crops or animals that could be tithed. Jesus did pay the Temple tax required of a Jewish man but made it clear to Peter that, as the Son of God, he was actually free of the requirements of such tribute.[46]

---

[45] Luke 2:22-24
[46] Matt.17:24-27

The Two Covenants

The only mention of tithing outside the gospels is in Hebrews, where the topic is the Old Covenant and the New Covenant. Anti-tithing arguments point to these verses as evidence that the Mosaic Covenant has passed away, and therefore tithing, which is related to it, has passed away also.

The passages which primarily discuss the two covenants are in Hebrews chapter 4 through chapter 10. A large portion of these verses emphasizes Jesus' role as a high priest. Heb. 4:14 starts us off: "Seeing then that we have a great high priest, that is passed into the heavens, Jesus the Son of God, let us hold fast our profession."

The high priesthood was established by God and specifies that the High Priest is of the lineage of Aaron.[47] Jesus' high priesthood was also established by God, but it was of the order of Melchizedek.[48] We are told that "For the priesthood being changed, there is made of necessity a change also of the law."[49]

The change in the priesthood is indicated by the fact that our new High Priest, Jesus, is definitely not of the tribe of Levi (Aaron's descendants) but is of the tribe of Judah.[50] What's more, the Levitical priesthood was based on a commandment, while the Melchizedek priesthood is based on the power of an endless life.[51]

What has not changed is that every high priest is ordained so that they might offer gifts and sacrifices to God. It was necessary then, that Jesus also offers a sacrifice, and the sacrifice he offered was himself.

Having done so, the second change in the law is now identified. Jesus presented an offering of the perfect sin sacrifice through an eternal

---

[47] Heb. 5:1-4
[48] Heb. 5:5-10; 6:20; 7:11
[49] Heb. 7:12
[50] Heb. 7:13-14
[51] Heb. 7:2-3; 15-16; 23-28

priesthood and not only is his ministry more excellent, but he is the mediator of a better covenant that is established upon better promises.

The first covenant wrote the law on stone, but the second covenant wrote it on hearts and minds.[52] The first covenant provided a temporary yet recurring means for sins and unrighteousness to be atoned for. The second covenant caused our sins to be forgiven once and for all.

The first covenant established a high priest to enter the Holy of Holies to stand before God for us. "The Holy Ghost this signifying, that the way into the holiest of all was not yet made manifest, while as the first tabernacle was yet standing."[53] Through his blood, Jesus ushered us all into the presence of God.

What's notable is that both covenants were required to be inaugurated by blood. The first covenant involved the blood of calves and goats sprinkled on the people and the book of the law.[54] The new covenant was inaugurated by the blood of Christ.[55] What has not changed is: "And almost all things are by the law purged with blood; and without shedding of blood is no remission."[56]

The final change is this: The Old Covenant did not have the power to make those who came before the altar perfect. In other words, it could not spiritually mature us to the point that it could deal with our consciences. Yes, our sin was forgiven. But the multiple sacrifices that were rendered over our lifetimes reminded us of our sins so that we always had an awareness of them.[57] But with just His one sacrifice, Jesus dealt with our sins forever! By the one offering, we were perfected and were able to stand before God righteous and with a clean conscience.[58]

---

[52] Jer. 31:31-34
[53] Heb. 9:8 King James Version
[54] Heb. 9:18-21
[55] Heb. 9:15-16
[56] Heb. 9:22
[57] Heb. 10:1-4
[58] Heb. 10:11-12; 22

The God of the First Covenant was unapproachable. Because of our sins and for our own protection, there had to be a gap that kept us from standing directly in His presence. But the God of the Second Covenant could be approached, the sins which separated us from him having been dealt with.[59]

Chapter 13 closes with admonishments as to behavior. We are encouraged toward brotherly love, hospitality, remembering the suffering, honoring marriage, contentment with what we have... I see all the lessons which the Law of Moses tried to instill in God's people still present and accounted for. But they are not spoken of as the law has been, a rulebook full of 'thou shall' and 'thou shall not's'.

My understanding of the letter to the Hebrews is that there was a change in the priesthood, and therefore a subsequent change in the law. Sacrifices for sin are no longer necessary since our High Priest Jesus, by his own blood, dealt with all our sins. But while guilt offerings and sin offerings and burnt offerings were brought to the altar for sins, a tithe, while it is a sacrifice of sorts, does not qualify as a sin offering.[60]

Jesus' once and for all sacrifice changed our status in God's sight to one of righteousness. And it does provide a framework for understanding any subsequent changes. But it does not answer my initial question: are we as post-resurrection Christians required to tithe as the Jews up to the time of Jesus did? Neither my pro-tithe stance nor my anti-tithe stance can claim this passage as proof for their position.

The Jerusalem Council

I do find a bit of an answer in an event called the Jerusalem Council. And it all started with a group of troublemakers called the Circumcision Faction. The apostle Paul discovered the Gentile believers were being told by certain Jewish believers that it wasn't enough to

---

[59] Heb. 12:18-24
[60] Heb. 10:8-10

believe in Jesus as the Christ, they also had to be circumcised as the Jews were in order to be truly saved.[61]

It got so bad that when Peter came to visit the church in Antioch, he was comfortable sitting and eating at a table with uncircumcised believers until the Jewish believers came to town. Then he suddenly wouldn't eat with the Gentiles anymore because of the pressure from this group.[62] Paul was livid.

What is interesting about circumcision is, like tithing, it was an established custom prior to the giving of the law. Both are easily argued thus: if a regulation was established prior to the law, then when the law was done away with, the earlier rules weren't included.

I have already learned that the entire law had not been done away with as I had thought. Rather, the changes that were made were in the priesthood and in the sacrifices for sin. As Jesus said, "Think not that I am come to destroy the law, or the prophets: I am not come to destroy, but to fulfill."[63] So none of the law has actually passed away. Instead, it has transformed into a new and better Covenant.

Things got so bad in Galatia that Paul and Barnabas finally took the problem to the leaders of the church in Jerusalem. After considering the arguments and noting the work of the Holy Spirit thus far in the body of Christ, the elders proclaimed the following judgment, delivered as a letter to the Gentile members of the church:

> "Since we have heard that some persons have gone out from us and troubled you with words, unsettling your minds, although we gave them no instructions ..."[64]

> "For it has seemed good to the Holy Spirit and to us to lay on you no greater burden than these requirements: that you abstain from what has been sacrificed to idols,

---

[61] Acts 15:1
[62] Gal. 2:11-13
[63] Matt. 5:17-18
[64] Acts 15:24; 28-29

and from blood, and from what has been strangled, and from sexual immorality. If you keep yourselves from these, you will do well. Farewell.

It is clear here that the Gentile church had not been commanded by either God or the church leaders to attempt to follow the Mosaic law in regards to circumcision. And having given it thought and by the leading of the Holy Spirit, the leaders identified the parts of the law that were most crucial and listed them in the letter.

I don't think it necessary to bring the law point by point before the Jerusalem elders. This incident seems to add to the argument that the tithe was not a requirement. If it remained vital it would have been mentioned in the letter. Paul did mention, however, "that we should remember the poor..."[65] And so they did.

The Early Church Gives...

It is in both Acts and II Corinthians that I finally find hard evidence of how the early church chose to give. The second chapter of Acts describes a fellowship of over 3,000 believers, all supporting each other. Each person considered what they possessed not their own, but that all things were common.[66] So much so that they regularly sold their possessions and from the proceeds it was distributed to every man as he had a need.

They met at the temple daily, and meals were frequently communal.

"...and great grace was upon them all."[67]

Because of this system, there was no one that lacked for anything. Those who possessed lands or houses (notice the plural, it indicates a surplus on the part of the owner) sold them, brought the

---

[65] Gal. 2:9-10
[66] Acts 2:44; 4:32
[67] Acts 4:33

price they received, and laid the money at the apostles' feet for distribution.

A man named Ananias and his wife Sapphira tried to get credit (spiritual credit, I guess) by holding back part of the money, yet pretending they were giving it all. Peter told them, "Look it was your land, right? And once you sold it the money was yours to do with as you pleased. So why did you lie?"[68]

After all, the believers weren't *required* to give the entire profit every time they sold a piece of property. They really weren't required to give any of it. It was evidence of a generosity of grace that moved those who gave to give.

...And Gives!

The story of the church at Corinth required me to dig up a bit more of a backstory. Near the end of his first letter to the Corinthians Paul noted that he had asked the churches of Galatia to take up a collection for the saints. He asks the Corinthian church to do so also.[69]

As a method of collection, he recommends that on the first day of every week, each of them should put something aside for this purpose, as God has prospered them. If they collected the gift this way, they could do so over time and not have to have a collection made when he arrived. His plan was to pass through Macedonia when he came to visit them. And when he arrived he would make arrangements to send their gift onward, accompanying it himself if necessary.

This gift is not a tithe, but rather a collection specifically for the poor. It's not clear what they were collecting: money, food, clothes? A little of everything?

In his second letter to the Corinthians, chapters 8 and 9, Paul starts off by telling them how generous the Macedonian church has

---

[68] Acts 5:1-4 (personal paraphrase)
[69] I Cor. 16:1-5

been.[70] In a time of extreme affliction, their abundant joy combined with their deep poverty somehow managed to overflow into some serious generosity! They gave not only what they had the power to give, but they went *beyond* what was in their power to give.

How did this happen? The Jewish New Testament Commentary puts it this way: "[Paul] stirs up the Corinthians' envy of virtue by presenting the congregations in nearby but competitive Macedonia (v.1) as a standard of comparison (v. 8). Despite trials and poverty they have been generous beyond their means without being nagged (vv. 2-3). They even pleaded for the privilege of giving (v. 4); further, their giving was not casual but an act of devotion to the Lord (vs. 5)".[71]

So first the Macedonian church gave themselves to the Lord, then they gave themselves to aiding Paul and his group, and then grace just overflowed into a generosity of giving!

Paul's purpose in mentioning them was to urge the Corinthians on in completing what they had promised so that they would not be embarrassed when he arrived. He'd already boasted about them to the Macedonians, telling them that the Corinthian church had been ready a year ago![72]

This is what I find most important in these two chapters. Paul had not commanded the Corinthians to give.[73] It had been their joy to offer to do so. They had taken on the task with a willing mind and he was encouraging them to demonstrate their sincerity by following through. So long as there was a readiness to do so, the results would be acceptable and would be based on what they had to give, not according to what they didn't have.[74]

---

[70] II Cor. 8:1-5

[71] Stern, David H., Jewish New Testament Commentary, p. 511, Jewish New Testament Publications, Inc. ©1992, 1996

[72] II Cor. 9:2-4

[73] II Cor. 8:8

[74] Ii Cor. 8:11-13

It wasn't his intent that the offering place an undue burden on them in order that other men's needs might be met. This flies in the face of the modern emphasis on sacrificial giving as being especially holy.

In fact, in the Code of Jewish Law is the following: "But he who has barely sufficient for his own needs is not obligated to give charity, for his own sustenance takes precedence over another's."

And then Paul noted that the church was living out something that was in the law, but it was not by commandment but by grace that they were moved! "As it is written, 'Whoever gathered much had nothing left over, and whoever gathered little had no lack.'"[75] The abundance the Corinthian church had would help those in need, and when abundance swung the other way, those believers would also help the Corinthians.

This reminds me of Eccl. 5:11: "When goods increase, they increase who eat them, and what advantage has their owner but to see them with his eyes?" In other words, no matter how much your crops multiply, a human being can only eat so much. At some point, the best you can do is watch while others eat the food you provided. This verse is tellingly paired with vs. 10: "He who loves money will not be satisfied with money, nor he who loves wealth with his income; this also is vanity."

So Paul encourages them. Every man should give as his heart purposes. Not grudgingly. Not because he has to. God loves a cheerful giver, and immovable commandments don't necessarily make for cheerful givers. God is able to fill you with grace for such good works.[76]

I find a key to Paul's discourse in II Cor. 9:12 – "For the ministry of this service is not only supplying the needs of the saints but is also overflowing in many thanksgivings to God."

This is where something clicks. First, these gifts and offerings weren't a means of supporting the church as an organization. The church as we know it today did not yet exist as an institution.

---

[75] II Cor. 8:15; Ex. 16:18
[76] II Cor. 9:7-8

Second, the goal of all this generosity and sharing of resources both here and in Acts 2 and 4 was to supply the needs of the saints so that they might glorify God. In our age, the church works very hard to supply the needs of those outside the church. And while this is all well and good, and certainly a way to demonstrate God's love to those who are lost, it seems we have forgotten our own brothers and sisters in Christ who are also in need.

Among the biblical examples of how New Covenant Christians conduct themselves is the following expectation: "Distributing to the necessity of saints; given to hospitality."[77] I'm not sure how we lost this act of love toward our own, but I feel we need to get it back.

While I was struggling to deal with my household's material needs on my own, I realized that the teachings I had received had a subtext. It seemed I had been taught that it was God's responsibility to take care of Christians, especially when they were tithers. We were to turn to God, not each other.

As a result, Christians weren't allowed to be poor. If we were poor, we must have been doing something wrong (like sinning and not tithing). Christians are somehow, by God's provision, supposed to all have the resources to take of themselves as well as the poor and needy of the whole world. Presumably, those poor and needy being helped were all non-believers. Yet Jesus said the poor would always be with us.[78]

In the Scriptures we are told to help those of our families who are in need rather than expect the church to do so.[79]

3 "Honor widows who are truly widows.

4 But if a widow has children or grandchildren, let them first learn to show godliness to their own household and to make some return to their parents, for this is pleasing in the sight of God.

---

[77] Rom. 12:13
[78] Matt. 26:11
[79] I Tim. 5:3

5 She who is truly a widow, left all alone, has set her hope in God and continues in supplications and prayers night and day,

6 but she who is self-indulgent is dead even while she lives.

7 Command these things as well, so that they may be without reproach. But if anyone does not provide for his relatives, and especially for members of his household, he has denied the faith and is worse than an unbeliever." (I Tim. 5:3-8)

When families determine to take care of their own then the church can focus on distributing their collected resources to the needy within the church who truly have no family to help. Jesus himself chided the religious leaders for using the traditions they built around the law to avoid their family obligations as directed by the law.

9 "And [Jesus] said to them, 'You have a fine way of rejecting the commandment of God in order to establish your tradition! **10** For Moses said, "Honor your father and your mother", and "Whoever reviles father or mother must surely die."

11 "But you say, 'If a man tells his father or his mother, "Whatever you would have gained from me is Corban," (that is, given to God) - **12** then you no longer permit him to do anything for his father or mother, thus making void the word of God by your tradition that you have handed down. And many such things you do."[80]

Or in modern terms, it is like telling our own parents, "I can't help you cover your mortgage or buy any food. All I have left right now is my tithe."

---

[80] Mark 7:9-12

81

A New Model of Giving?

I don't foresee the worldwide church going back to a system of having all things in common. But it would be nice to see us go back to a way of giving that is based not on regulations, but on the grace brought by the New Covenant.

This starts with a giving that is focused on taking care of our brothers and sisters in Christ. First, by reminding each other that taking care of our families is a priority, even over being generous for the offering plate. Second, by establishing ministries that focus on congregational members so that they have no lack. This would allow those who have more than they need at the moment to spread their blessing.

This type of giving is based on a grace resulting in an eagerness to give. I imagine a church where giving isn't a requirement, but rather a result of a heart being moved. The willing mind comes first, and out of such a person gives according to how God has blessed them. Sometimes they will have an abundance. Sometimes not so much. But in the end, there is a balance of things.

As much as I would love to give that way now, I know that for the most part, money that I put into an offering plate is not likely to reach the needy *within* the church. And because a church organization has its own expenses, only in the mega-churches can a large portion of funds actually reach the needy outside the church walls.

This has never stopped the Holy Spirit, however. As Jonathan once said, "...there is no restraint to the Lord to save by many or by few."[81] I have always known those who will press money or food or clothes into a brother or sister's hand and simply say, "God told me you needed this."

When I was living with my family in Japan, I checked the bank account one payday, the day money is supposed to be deposited *into* the account, and realized there was nothing there! Everything had somehow been pre-spent and when the check went in, it pretty much evaporated.[82]

---

[81] I Sam. 14:6b

I was alone with my children and desperate. Forget paying the bills! What are we going to eat for the next two weeks?! As I was sitting there, panic-stricken, there was suddenly there was a knock on the door.

Joseph Jenkins, a brother in Christ from the base chapel, was standing on my doorstep holding a bag full of groceries. He said the Lord told him we needed it. God had to have told him before I even found out.

I could have cried. Let me tell you, Bro. Jenkins had never just popped over to our house before. I was more in the habit of talking with his wife, LaDeidre. Joe only visited when both of our families were hanging out together.

There have been times when I have been the one sharing what I had with a fellow Christian. Those times when I looked at someone and the thought came into my mind, "You really should give them a little money." Those times when I heard someone needed food and I found a way to get a little food or money to them. And there have been times when it was myself and my family who have been the recipient of an unexpected and much-needed gift.

He that gathered much had nothing over, and he that gathered little had no lack.

---

[82] A long and involved story which I won't tell here.

Chapter Seven

Beyond the Tithe

Paul's letter to the Romans is the Bible's best explanation of the gospel and how it transforms the believer from being someone bound to sin and death, and thus subject to the law, into a person dead to sin but alive unto God. And the difference is Jesus.[83]

"But now we are released from the law, having died to that which held us captive, so that we serve in the new way of the Spirit and not in the old way of the written code."[84] We still serve God, but there's something new going on.

Romans 8:1-2 reemphasizes this. "There is therefore now no condemnation for those who are in Christ Jesus. For the law of the Spirit of life has set you free in Christ Jesus from the law of sin and death."

This does not mean merely that we are free from our overwhelming tendency to sin. We are also free from the consequences

---

[83] Rom. 6:7,11; 7:1-4
[84] Rom. 7:6

of sin which the Mosaic law spells out. Both the law and our consciences condemned us. The purpose of the law was to tutor us and to direct us to the coming Messiah. When Jesus came, his death and resurrection brought us entirely to the goal.

As Paul winds up his explanation of the law, the gospel, and how Jesus has brought us into a better place, he gives us, beginning with chapter 12, a look at how those who are dead to sin should conduct themselves. Indeed, it is summed up best by saying, "Owe no one anything except to love each other, for the one who loves another has fulfilled the law." And also, "Love does no wrong to a neighbor: therefore, love is the fulfilling of the law."[85]

Jesus himself, even before his death, directed us beyond the law from the very beginning of his ministry in his discourse, the Sermon on the Mount. In Matt. 5:17-20 Jesus speaks of a fulfillment of the law (vs.17) and a higher righteousness (vs.20). He tells his listeners, "For I tell you, unless your righteousness exceeds that of the scribes and Pharisees, you will never enter the kingdom of heaven."

Exceeds?! Really? Now in Jesus' day, nobody could out-righteous the scribes and the Pharisees. They were the most righteous people around. They set the gold standard for righteousness! Scribes were experts in God's written word and their job was to not only copy the Torah but to teach and interpret it. They knew the law better than anyone. As for the Pharisees, they were "quite concerned with the proper keeping of the Sabbath, tithing, and purification rituals."[86]

And Jesus said we have got to do better than that? You can almost see the crowd around him looking at each other in astonishment. But then Jesus gave examples of what he meant. He starts each section by quoting the law, "You have heard that it was said to those of old..." and then following it up with the higher standard, "But I say to you..."

---

[85] Rom. 13:8,10
[86] Holman Bible Dictionary, Holman Bible Publishers, ©1991, p. 790.

Example 1 (Matt. 5:21-26):

The Law: You have heard "You shall not murder; and whoever murders shall be liable to judgment."

Beyond the Law: But I say to you that everyone who is angry with their brother will be liable to judgment. Whoever insults his brother will be liable to the (Jewish) council, but whoever says "You fool!" will be liable to the hell of fire.

Before you present your offering to God, if someone has a problem with you, go be reconciled with them first. Get right with them, then worship God.

Well! That's certainly a much higher standard than simply refraining from murdering someone.

Example 2 (Matt. 5:27-32):

The Law: You have heard it said, "You shall not commit adultery."

Beyond the Law: But I say to you, if you're looking at a woman with lust, you're committing adultery right then and there in your heart, even if your body is not yet involved. If your eyes, your hands, or even your thoughts are prone to sin, you need to deal with it. It's better to deal with it here and now than go to hell for it later.

Example 3 (Matt. 5:31-32):

The Law: It has been said, "Whoever wants to put away his wife must give her a bill of divorce." (So the Law does allow you to get a divorce.)

Beyond the Law: But I say to you, if you divorce your wife for any reason less than sexual infidelity, you force her and whoever marries her afterward into a position of adultery, because she committed no offense against her first marriage vows. So although you did righteously according to the Law, you really were unrighteous.

Example 4 (Matt. 5:38-42):

The Law: You have heard it said, "An eye for an eye, and a tooth for a tooth."

Beyond the Law: But I say to you, don't resist evil. If someone hits you on the right cheek, turn the other cheek to him also. If they sue you for your coat, give them your cloak also.

Then Jesus really brings it on home.

Example 5 (Matt. 5:43-48):

The Law: You have heard it said, "Love your neighbor and hate your enemy."

Beyond the Law: But I say to you, Love your enemy. Bless those that curse you. Do good to those that hate you. Pray for those which despitefully use you. Pray for those who persecute you.

That is a complete turnaround from permission to hate your enemy!

Now I'm really starting to understand. I take this new insight and look at what the law said concerning the tithe, and then try to think it forward. The law told those who stewarded that which God brought forth in Israel, the fruit of the ground and that which was born of the herds, to tithe of it to the Temple. Its purpose included supporting the Levitical priesthood, providing assistance to the poor and was part of one's fellowship with God as you sat at His table.

If I am going to exceed the original Levitical definition of the tithe, then I must strive to stop seeing tithing as the highest standard of righteousness in giving, and seek to go beyond the tithe. What does that mean to me?

Boaz comes to mind as an example. According to the law, the owner of a field was not to reap to the very edge of the field. Neither was he to return after he harvested and go over the field again, picking up what had fallen to the ground behind the harvesters. This food was to be left for the use of the poor. It was for those who had no fields of their own, nor the resources to buy the food when it reached the market. They would be permitted to follow behind the harvesters in another citizen's fields and gather what they could.

In theory, you could leave a teeny-tiny bit of grain stalks standing on the far edges of your field. You could instruct your harvesters to get everything they could and be extra careful not to drop too much. So long as your workers didn't return over the same ground, you could count yourself obedient to the letter of the law.

But the purpose of the law is to train in righteousness. And the law of Moses shows us the heart of God. Our God is a God who is concerned about the widow and the orphan. This is a God who desires to feed the needy with the bounty of the earth that He himself brings forth year after year. To obey the letter of the law might make you look righteous in the sight of man, but if you haven't divined the intents of the Spirit behind the law, you're missing out on the heart of God.

When Boaz saw this foreign woman, Ruth, gleaning behind his harvesters, he was moved by a spirit of compassion and by a generous heart. He made inquiries as to who she was and found out this stranger was loyal and loving to a kinswoman of his. And so he told his workers,

"Let her glean even among the sheaves, and do not reproach her. And also pull out some from the bundles for her and leave it for her to glean, and do not reproach her."[87] What's more, Boaz instructed Ruth to stick close to his reapers where she wouldn't be harassed (being a single

---

[87] Ruth 2:15-16

Beyond the Tithe | Valerie R Jackson

woman with no male protector) and invited her to eat her midday meal out of what was provided for his workers.

When Ruth returned home that evening, not only did her labors produce an unusually generous amount of grain for their household needs, but she gave her mother-in-law some of the food left over from her lunch. Boaz had provided so much she couldn't eat it all, and was able to bring some home.

Boaz went beyond the requirements of the law, and his actions were borne of compassion for a fellow human being.

Love is the fulfillment of the Law.[88]

So how do I, how do we, find a way to go beyond the tithe?

First, I need to recognize the importance of love in all my actions. It doesn't matter if I'm giving, praying, or baking cookies. It's about other people, not myself.

Second, I must resolve not to let the law limit how I give, how much I give, what I give, or to whom I give. Any sort of quota now strikes me as a limitation. Why should I stop at 10% when I am in a season of abundance? I also see that any awareness of 10% as a minimum that I should give also takes my joy away when I cannot meet what I perceive of as divine expectation.

If a family member has a need, what I had planned to give for the needs of the church is no longer *Corban*.[89] I can help them with a free conscience. If I leave town and visit a different church to worship with other believers, I can give happily without feeling I am taking something away from my 'home' church. It's also quite likely that a visitor to my own church sees fit to present an offering before the Lord there.

Knowing that I am free from such legal constraints means I can turn my mind instead to following the leadings of the Holy Spirit. Has a homeless person crossed my path? Do I discover a Christian family I

---

[88] Rom. 13:10
[89] Meaning "a gift devoted or given to God."

89

worship with needs a little help with the groceries at the same time my hens are at their laying peak? Does my church need to replace the roof? Does a family member need to share my shelter for a little bit? I can help.

Third, I must continually remind myself that everything in my life has already been devoted to God. That's just part of being a Christian. I think of Him when I arise and appreciate the day. I put my time on hold to pray to Him when someone has a need.

Giving, then, (whether to support the work of the church or to alleviate the pressures of life for others), is not something special I do because I am righteous. Distributing resources are a part of my life as much as anything else I invite God into. It is no longer a legal requirement, and abruptly becomes part of the joy of just living in His presence.

Fourth, just as I ask for His help to direct me when my resources run low, I want to train myself to keep an eye out for fellow believers who have a need when I have an abundance. Sharing with others is now on the agenda! "Give and it shall be given unto you"[90] becomes about reciprocity, not getting God on the ropes so I can get something from him.

> "Let him ... labor, doing honest work with his own hands, so that he may have something to share with anyone in need."[91]

> "... Whoever has two tunics is to share with him that has none, and whoever has food is to do likewise."[92]

And I always go back to this, which I think has become my favorite verse in this whole study: "As it is written, He that had gathered much had nothing over; and he that had gathered little had no lack."

---

[90] Luke 6:38a
[91] Eph. 4:28
[92] Luke 3:11b

Lastly, I always want to remember my own struggles with this issue and recognize that tithing was, when all was said and done, an attempt to manage my finances by manipulating God. When it came to my daily bread, I lived afraid. It was only when I realize that God delights in me, and He already knows what I need for life, that I can let go of the fear and walk in freedom. Lack vs abundance stops being the issue. Because God has me, I can let it go.

Chapter Eight

My Yoke is Easy

The most difficult part of grasping a new spiritual truth is in changing your mindset. I told you I blew off what I was learning twice before I finally gave it serious consideration. Having been conditioned to give to God with an expectation of receiving something bigger in return, it became hard to give without the thought passing through my mind, no matter how fleeting, that there will be an earthly payoff. I sometimes still have to shoo that thought away, but it gets easier to do so every time.

True freedom in giving means we're able to give, whether to the church or to the needy, without an ulterior motive, without an agenda. Once we are free from the bondage of worry, or of greed, our choices suddenly become wide open.

As Jesus said, "Enter by the narrow gate. For the gate is wide and the way is easy that leads to destruction, and those who enter by it are many. For the gate is narrow and the way is hard that leads to life, and those who find it are few."[93]

---

[93] Matt. 7:13-14

Having entered by the narrow gate (Jesus) and traversed the rocky path that puts self to death, it is as if the path abruptly ended in a meadow full of wildflowers and I'm giddily running around, conscious of every colorful, beckoning bloom! Beyond the law and beyond the bondage of sin there stretches before me a field of freedom!

The problem was never about whether a believer should have money. The problem was the way money so often gets a grip on the believer. And the chains binding you when money is your god chafe just as hard on the haves as the have-nots. Setting your mind on things above means not being focused on struggling your way through life or building your personal empire, but rather moving forward because you have got heaven in your sights.

"Where your treasure is, that's where your heart is,"[94] And in terms of eternity, it is an utter waste of time to have your heart grasping at earthly things that you know you aren't going keep anyway. That's the message Jesus was trying to get across to the rich young man.[95] He truly sought God, but material things and social privilege had him shackled to the here and now.

Jesus wanted him to know, "Your heart is aiming too low! Let me free it to aim higher." If you follow the encounter between Jesus and this privileged young man to its end, you'll see Jesus pointing toward a future inheritance to his disciples. Peter, speaking for the disciples, said that they had given up everything to follow Jesus. What will there be for us? And Jesus spoke of the time of regeneration and an inheritance of eternal life. That's certainly of more value than anything we can acquire during our few days on earth.

Jesus also said of the scribes and Pharisees of his day, "They tie up heavy burdens, hard to bear, and lay them on people's shoulders, but they themselves are not willing to move them with their finger."[96] But of himself, Jesus said, "Come unto me, all who labor and are heavy laden,

---

[94] Matt. 6:21
[95] Matt. 19:16-30; Mark 10:17-31
[96] Matt. 23:4

and I will give you rest. Take my yoke upon you, and learn from me, for I am gentle and lowly in heart, and you will find rest for your souls. For *my* yoke is easy, and *my* burden is light."[97]

I love the easy yoke! The demands of the world that used to beat me down are now a 'light and momentary trouble.'[98] The demands of the Law of Moses that I thought kept me bound turned out to be the tutor that brought me to freedom.

When we move past the tithes and offerings required by the law, and step toward generosity and remembering the poor, there is no longer any biblical mandate for Christian giving. That gives us total freedom to give as our heart's desire and as the Spirit leads us.

Because we have entered through the narrow gate, and because we have entered into a New Covenant where God's word is inscribed on our hearts, we no longer have sinful motivations driving our choices. And without the compulsion of a tithe that was never supposed to limit our giving, our hearts have room to become even more expansive.

Reasons for Giving

There are several very wonderful reasons for giving generously, some of which were mentioned back in Chapter 2 in regards to tithing.

1) **Some people simply love to give!** These are those who have hearts filled with compassion. They see a hurt, they want to alleviate it. They see a need, they want to fill it. They see a purpose, they want to join with it.

Of all of us who give, those in whom the Holy Spirit tends to manifest in works of compassion and generosity will probably be the giddiest when they start walking in freedom. It will be like a door being flung open, like a dam bursting. There are no constraints to the tasks for their open hands.

---

[97] Matt. 11:28-30, emphasis mine
[98] II Cor. 4:17

94

They no longer have to determine what's left after they give what they are required to give. They can go where the need is greatest or toward their heart's desire.

2) **Some Christians are dedicated supporters of the church.** They give to the church because they see that as the best way to spread the love of Christ and support the mission of the church. They know that churches aren't built on air and angels' wings. Even Jesus had a home base in Capernaum.

They are like the women who followed Jesus and his disciples, supporting them out of their own resources.[99] They are the 'Martha's' of the body of Christ who keep the lights on, the soup in the Soup Kitchen and make sure missionaries have airline tickets to and from their destination. They hold down the fort when the soldiers of God go forth. And they make sure the fort is still standing when they come back home.

3) **Some Christians have a determination to make God's will happen.** Giving is their joy because their life is a life that takes seriously every leading of the Holy Spirit. They don't need to understand God's purposes. And they don't worry about their own needs. They know all that is in God's hands.

These are the sheep who, when they hear their master's voice, follow trustingly. These are the ones most tuned to the Spirit's guidance. They provision others with a randomness that seems out of the blue. They approach someone they don't know because God asked them to give them a specific amount of money. They just happen to be at church with some extra funds in their pocket on the Sunday that special offering is taken up for that family in crisis.

When my husband and I drove to Kansas to visit my son's family, just as we were filling the tank in the car to head back to Virginia, the lady in the vehicle next to us started chatting us up about our trip. We were using a map printout from the internet and state maps to navigate.

---

[99] Luke 8:1-3

The next thing we knew she rushed to her car, pulled out a GPS, and pressed it on us. God had told her to give it to us.

Now my husband kept telling her "No, thank you. We are okay." But in the end, because she pressed us, we allowed her to give us this gift. We had never used one before, but I wondered, as I tinkered with it and waited to get on the road, why God thought we needed a GPS. Sure enough, on the way home the turn signals on the car quit working. That GPS was instrumental in our easing safely into the correct lanes well before our exits came up.

4) **Some will give because their obedience to God set their feet on that path.** They don't really need a spiritual reason to give or even a heartfelt urge. God's Word indicates they should support the ministry, and help the poor, sick, widows and orphans. It's what Christians do, and they are Christians. So they do it without stressing about it.

Their true spiritual focus is probably elsewhere. They're busy doing God's work, whether behind the scenes in administrative duties or out in the field with missionary work. They could be teaching for the children's ministry at church, or training up their own youngsters in God's way at home. Living for God is a lifestyle and everything they do relates to Him.

Ways to Give

The following are some ways in which the Christian can give. These are just options. Surely your particular circumstances might drive you to think even more creatively. But overall I'm grouping them into Systemic Giving vs. Non-systemic Giving.

A Clear Plan

Some believers have a preference for orderly and systemic giving. They like to give the same thing at the same time, every time. And

I have to agree, if your income is stable, having a system certainly simplifies things, leaving you to put your brain cells to other uses. It also can be the best way for those who have a set amount always available on set days to distribute it. For instance, salaries, automatic payments, etc.

One method is to give a certain percentage from every paycheck. Now, I know by now you may be thinking I'm urging you to avoid giving 10% at all costs. But we're not talking tithing, we're talking walking in freedom here. Which means 10% is still do-able. The virtue of giving 10% is that it's fast and easy to calculate. You could just as easily, depending on your circumstances, choose 5% or 20%. Or 32.7% if you're a math whiz and just like the challenge.

Another way is to decide upon a certain amount that you always want to give every time. Based upon your resources you may decide $20 every week is do-able. Or "this year I'm giving $150 per paycheck, and if I get a bonus this year I'd like to give a flat amount of money from that, too."

Don't feel locked into your choice. Being locked in is the opposite of walking about freely, and God sure loves that cheerful giver. If circumstances change you could adjust your giving up or down. If an emergency occurs, you can change it entirely, knowing you can go back to your preferred method at any time.

And there are other benefits to consistently giving a calculated amount. First, your church will receive a dependable source of income from you. For the sake of the finance committee who has to do accounting and budgeting, dependable resources are a really nice thing to have. Second, consistency will eventually equal quantity. Some people are not able to give $100 or $1,000 at a shot. But just like persistent savings, persistent giving will eventually add up to an amount that pleases you.

Third, determining what you give, when you give it, and how and where you give it only has to happen once. After the decisions are made, you can put your giving on a mental autopilot and your gifts are assured.

The only disadvantage I can see is that giving your offering can also easily become rote, or even invisible if you use an automatic debit system. You will miss the joy of deliberately bringing your gift before the Lord. If this bothers you, you may need to take steps to keep your giving active. For instance, you might do periodic reviews of what you give in order to keep your mind engaged in the process.

You could also write checks; archaic, I know, but it's a very deliberate process that takes a few minutes focus. As a wild idea of an example: Suppose every Saturday evening you sit down in a favorite spot, thank God for this week's blessings, write a check and formally present it to Him, telling Him it will be your joy to put it in the offering plate tomorrow morning. Not only did you have a time of communion with God, you probably could hardly wait to jump up and get to church the next day, just so you could hand your offering over.

E-giving may also need to be managed if you want to avoid a spiritual disconnect with your giving. Just as going shopping with a credit card does not have the same mental impact as standing and counting the cash in your wallet out on the counter, swiping your debit card at the church kiosk may also not be as fulfilling a way to re-distribute what God has provided for you.

A Matter of Flexibility

Others may find non-systemic giving works better for them. It allows for moves of the Spirit and shifts in income. For those with hourly wages, especially when their work or hours change seasonally, and their expenses do not, making a decision on giving based on what's in their pocket each week is probably less hazardous to their household budget.

The chronically underemployed can probably expect gaps in their giving, with times of relative abundance balanced by times of fewer available resources. When my husband was doing landscaping and I was in retail, his work picked up dramatically between May and November, and my hours increased from May right through the holiday season.

You'll notice I didn't say anything about January - April. That's where the gap came in our incomes.

People who work in fields like the housing market can also expect vast swings, though we're talking good and bad years rather than months. Teachers routinely get a summer break from their paychecks. Farmers get paid when the crops go in. Teenagers may only work during the summer. The momentarily unemployed are dealing with the financial swing between having a job and not having a job. And any time you have a gap in income, you have several months when you're playing financial catch up before things stabilize.

It's these believers who are instructed particularly to give out of their means as God has blessed them. When they *can* give, they do so with a heartfelt thankfulness that they *have* something to give. I can't stress enough how close you can sometimes feel to God when your charitable giving is never allowed to become business as usual. And when you're down to the widow's mite sort of giving,[100] just as she did, you can put your trust in God without guilt over the suitability of your offering.

When you find you are not in a position to give at all, then you simply put it all on hold for a bit. It's not going to stop God's love for you or yours for Him. And when that window of opportunity does open up, you can give gladly and in whichever direction you choose. More frequently, those who don't have extra resources often are the ones who find other ways to show our love for the body of Christ during these times.

Christians who are sensitive to the direction of the Holy Spirit may also desire to not make any advance decisions on their gifts. This week they put money into the offering plate to help with the everyday needs of the church. Next week they give a little less because they ran into Brother So-and-so who needed a new battery for his car so he could get to his job. This summer the church was sending out missionaries, so they add a little extra in to contribute to that. Right before Christmas

---

[100] Luke 21:1-4

they receive a bonus sufficient to deal with the church's sudden plumbing issues.

For believers such as these, giving based on self-imposed quotas just gets in their way!

Making the Change

As I pointed out earlier, after going years, for some of us decades, believing that the tithe was the only God-sanctioned way to give, it takes a little work to retrain our minds. Fortunately, that's what Scripture is for. Transformation of our minds is brought about by meditation on the Word of God.

In other words, when I give and the thought comes into my mind that I'm supposed to get a hundredfold return for my giving or some such nonsense, I throw some Scripture at it. Just like Jesus proclaimed, "It is written...!" when the devil tempted him.

My Brain: Malachi 3:9 says I'm cursed with a curse because I'm robbing God if I don't tithe.

The Spirit: *Galatians 3:13, which was written after the resurrection of Jesus, also says Christ has redeemed us from the curse of the law.*

My Brain: My church will judge me as not spiritually mature. I may have to leave my ministry.

The Spirit: *Remember Colossians 2:16-17. Let no man judge you in terms of following the Law of Moses. They were a shadow of what was to come. You reside in the New Covenant of the Son, not in the shadow of the Law.*

For those who have limited resources, let me say this boldly: God has never required you to tithe! And he doesn't require you to empty your pockets every time you come to church. Anything you may choose to give, count it joyfully as a love letter to the Lord.

For all of us, there's no need to manipulate God by our giving. His love for us was complete before we gave anything. His love is complete even if we can't give. As with God's dealings with the patriarch Jacob, his desire to care for us doesn't come with a monetary stipulation. We take care of our children because we love them. And God takes care of His for the same reason.

The truth does indeed set us free. But if the Word falls on ground where we've already got something growing, sometimes we have to do some weeding to give it room to set roots. To make the change in my heart, not just in my head, I did have to move away from giving exactly 10%. I also had to start thinking more holistically. Everything that I do circles around God. Giving isn't something special or extra.

To church leaders who want their church to throw off the yoke of the doctrine of tithing, I encourage you to encourage yourselves by looking ahead to a body of Christ where everyone gives as God has blessed them, and no one gives out of guilt. I know it will be tough. I'm a teacher myself, and it's embarrassing to publicly admit when I've blown it. But this isn't a teaching I feel I can keep to myself. It's hard to skip about merrily in the Promised Land when you know your brothers and sisters are still in toiling in the land of slavery.

I'm already thinking of the difficulties involved in implementing a teaching that, in the eyes of much of the church, is radical and downright dangerous. They might wonder how they could cover the bills if people aren't encouraged to tithe.

Remind yourself that 100% of your congregation isn't tithing anyway. If you've got more than 8% you should probably be amazed. (According to a Barna Group poll, only 8% of Protestants and 2% of Catholics actually give a full 10% of their income to the church.)[101] We may as well set the other 92% free. And cut the tithing minority free while we're at it. If they are tithers now, they'll probably astonish us with their God-given ability to give generously without coercion.

---

[101] https://www.barna.org/barna-update/congregations/41-new-study-shows-trends-in-tithing-and-donating#

Also, remind yourself that the doctrine of tithing is a minority position in the church, not the universal teaching we may have thought it was. There's a good chance we can find support from other church leaders as we make the journey.

It occurs to me that encouraging tithing because we as a church are fearful of not being able to keep our lights on... well, that's probably a serious lack of faith on our part. Do I really think the kingdom of God is going to come to a screeching halt? (I'm trying to imagine that right now, and I'm really amused at my presumption. The church has survived 2000 years. Do I really believe I have the power to bring it all crashing down and blow God's plans for eternity?)

At the church I currently attend, a particularly urgent need once came up. Instead of asking for each member to give $20 or $30 as once was their custom, they simply told us what the problem was, how much money was needed to solve it, and asked us to each give according to what was in our hearts. Then they took up an offering. I was delighted the next Sunday when they announced that the amount collected was within a couple of dollars of what they had asked for.

This has happened a few other times, and I no longer believe we need to shakedown our membership in order to go forth with the work of the Lord.

If your church is dying, lack of money is probably not what's killing it. If it's vibrant, lack of money isn't going to stop it.

There will be those who will fight this teaching. Expect it. And know that it is quite all right. Remember, part of being free is allowing others their own freedom in Christ. If they feel conviction in their hearts when they don't tithe, and they are satisfied to continue to give in such a manner, there is no reason to mess them up by insisting they change their mindset. Tithing is not a sin, it's just an unnecessary adherence to a

Law that has already been transformed. Nobody's salvation is riding on this.

In fact, to have a *"The Spirit says"* backup verse to what The Brain is going to shortly be telling you, try re-reading the 14th chapter of Romans and then the very first verse of Romans 15. It reminds us we don't want to put a stumbling-block in a brother's way by insisting they believe the way we believe on what is obviously going to be a debatable matter. To do so is not acting in love.

For both the brother who chooses to tithe and the brother who chooses not to; for the one who believes God desires one thing, and another who is just as sure God allows something completely opposite; if you stand before God as His obedient servant, and your heart is only set on pleasing God, then you both do well. Let it remain between you and your God.

Challenge to the Church

I would like to challenge the church, as the body of Christ as well as individual believers, to look into ways we might return to ways of giving that help our brothers and sisters first. The office of deacon was originally established to deal more fairly with distributing resources to the widows, so we have our biblical example.

It's not enough just to set up a Food Pantry, though that is certainly a step in the right direction. Members should be encouraged to contribute to it and use it without embarrassment, and not always see it as an outreach ministry for the community rather than a resource for the church.

In Acts 6:1 it was noted that the distribution to the widows was daily. So we shouldn't be surprised when some of today's members will need regular assistance rather than intermittent. Sometimes people just need to get over a gap. But for others the struggle is ongoing, a generational or systemic problem, because what is coming in for their household is insufficient.

In addition to supplying basic needs, it may also be good to help our brothers and sisters move forward financially. This may require offering financial education for those who need and desire it. But it may also be a matter of providing opportunities. One year our church offered help for people seeking their GED, assisting with the process and paying the test fee for them when they were ready.

If someone is aware of an opportunity, whether in education or the workforce, should they not give those in their church a head's up? Even more, if someone is hiring, they might find the person they need in the pew next to them.

There is a saying, "Give a man a fish and you feed him for a day. Teach a man to fish and you feed him for a lifetime."

Some people like to give a man a fish. They know he needs to eat today while someone else is busy carving out a fishing pole for him. They keep food pantries full, but they are just as likely to show up at someone's house with homemade meals, hot from the oven. ("I made extra.")

Some people delight in teaching a man to fish. They'll walk a friend through every step of the fishing process if you ask them to, and have their phone on standby if any questions arise while you are standing on the dock.

Some people prefer to dig a pond and stock it. And then invite others to come fish in it. If their community needs more jobs, they will be the first looking to bring an industry in suited to the skills of those most in need. Some people will even show *you* how to dig a pond! And then help you start your own fishing industry. These are entrepreneurs who love to create other entrepreneurs. Sometimes we just don't know what skills and contacts are walking around in our churches!

There is no one way to achieve this. As with any form of giving, the greatest pleasure and joy is to walk in freedom and according to the move of the Spirit and the dictates of your heart. Once the home cooks, compulsive teachers, and cheerful entrepreneurs have finished their tasks, many are the needs that will be met.

It is important that we stop seeing our fellow believers as someone God is going to take care of if they just have enough faith, and hold a hand out ourselves. We need to make them a priority.

"If a brother or sister is poorly clothed and lacking in daily food, and one of you says to them, 'Go in peace, be warmed and filled,' without giving them the things needed for the body, what good is that?"[102]

Remember, Boaz had the resources, but he didn't just give Ruth a generous lunch. He shored up her dignity by giving her the opportunity to work for herself in his own fields.

We, also, should help the needy outside the church walls, but not at the expense of our own Christian brothers. We ought to be able to do the one without neglecting the other. Especially if we work together!

Most of all I want to encourage every believer to have the courage to walk in freedom and love enough to encourage their brothers and sisters to do the same. We will each draw closer to God in our own way, and yet we can still be on one accord in love.

Beyond the law there is a place of freedom where joy grows and grows. Beyond the land of rules and regulations there is another land, a kingdom where grace itself abounds and the generous rejoice. Through the narrow gate and beyond the horizon there is a field of wildflowers, where every beckoning bloom has its own glorious possibilities.

To all I wish you Godspeed as you continue to grow - Beyond the Tithe.

---

[102] James 2:15-16

About the Author

Valerie R Jackson began her ministry as a Bible Instructor in 2001 while attending the Inspirational Services at the Misawa AB chapel in Japan. By the time she left she was conducting weekly Bible Studies for the Protestant Women of the Chapel ministry.

Upon returning to the U.S. she attended Abilene Christian University in Texas for a year in order to complete her Bachelor's degree, and while she was there obtained a minor in Biblical Studies. When she moved to Charlottesville, VA she became a Bible Instructor for the First Baptist Church Adult Sunday School, including a stint as a course teacher for Transformation Ministries International L.E.A.D. classes. She is currently moving toward developing a Bible Study course for couples at her church.

Valerie is a Christian fine artist as well as author of the blog, Off-Kilter Bible Studies. She lives with her husband Johnny R. Jackson Sr. in Louisa, VA.

Acknowledgements

Thank you to my husband, Johnny R. Jackson, Sr, for his willing enthusiasm in debating theology with me. My life with you is so much fun!

Thank you to my talented daughter, Tiffani V. S. Bowe, for the resources of Graphics.tif. She created the cover design and even made the little Off-Kilter Bible studies logo look just like I wanted it to.

Thanks also to the leaders of First Baptist Church on 7th and Main of Charlottesville, VA; Pastor Hodari K. Hamilton. M.Div and his wife Rev. Khadijah Hamilton, M.Div, for their continuous encouragement to their oddball Bible instructor, even when her Bible lessons went off the beaten path and into uncharted territory.

Thanks to my parents, Rev. and Mrs. Will C. Tabron, for giving me a solid lifelong foundation in the Word of God. I love Him because you loved Him.

Much love to my son Anthony, Jr for his brilliance in finding and successfully courting his lovely wife, Ursala. They have given me three loving grandchildren; Deion, Amara and Averi. Love also to my deep-thinker son Marcus, because of who God made him to be. To my stepson Joseph, another seeker and searcher, to his big brother Johnny Jr. And to Tiny Johnny, beloved and gifted grandson.

May God bless you and keep you all.

Made in the USA
Monee, IL
13 September 2023

42710800R00059